LET THERE BE LIGHT
Parish Leadership for the 21st Century

FATHER JAMES GRANT

Modotti Press

Dedicated to my wife Dolores

Special thanks to Richard Alston for his support and Interest in all my work

In grateful remembrance of:

Mary Wood
Fr Neville McKie
Fr Vernon Collins

Published in 2016 by Connor Court Publishing Pty Ltd

Copyright © James Grant

All rights reserved. No part of this book may be reproduced or transmitted in any form or by any means, electronic or mechanical, including photocopying, recording or by any information storage and retrieval system, without prior permission in writing from the publisher.

Connor Court Publishing Pty Ltd.
PO Box 224W
Ballarat VIC 3350
sales@connorcourt.com
www.connorcourt.com

ISBN: 978-1-925138-99-3

Printed in Australia

Front Cover   Depicts the southern entrance of St James Catholic Church Brighton – damaged by fire in 2015. Photograph by Vincent Azzopardi

What are they saying about 'Let there be Light'

This book confronts the need for change in the Catholic Church.

I have known the author of this book Father James Grant for over 10 years and consider him a courageous and strong religious leader. Father James is a visionary and personal friend. He is an authentic Church leader who believes in taking the Catholic Church to the people and not the other way around.

Father James first came to my attention when I was the Director of Human Resources at AIG which is a multi-national insurance organisation. He was introduced to me by then AIG Chief Executive Officer Mr. Chris Townsend who described him as: "an entrepreneurial and interesting priest". He was right on both counts!

Father James founded the organisation "Chaplains without Borders" in 2004 to provide chaplaincy services to corporate Australia. Father James was appointed as the world's first chaplain to the casino industry in 2006 (Crown Casino).

Father James provides an insightful view of the need for change to current parish practices and strategy in this book. He talks about the need for ministers to move outside what he describes as their "comfort zone". Father James argues that if a parish fails to adapt or reform it is at serious risk of decline.

He uses his knowledge and experience gained over many years in business and provides parish ministers with a framework for leading effective change in their parishes. He explores a range of concepts and strategies which will assist a parish to implement the necessary change to survive and thrive into the future.

Father James believes that the Church is just like any other organisation. It must stay focused on and relevant to the needs of its community or stakeholders to thrive and grow. It must therefore adapt to new ways of doing things and engaging with its community and/or stakeholders.

This book is compelling reading for parish leaders involved in managing stakeholders and setting the strategic direction of the parish. He encourages Church leaders to fully understand the demographics of the community or stakeholders it serves, to be open minded to new ideas without compromising on Church values or belief's and to use the sphere of influence to drive real outcomes whilst being tolerant of the diversity of views held by the community and stakeholders.

Father James wants the Catholic Church to make a difference in the lives of people through renewal.

*--***Carlo Galati,** *Former National General Manager AIG Human Resources*

I have worked with Father James for many years through the 'Chaplain's without Borders' pastoral care program he has provided to our workplace. I admire the work undertaken by Father James and the contemporary way he seeks to add value to the lives of many and in parallel, works to make the church relevant in this 21st century. Father James understands that the concept of a congregation has moved beyond attendance at a Sunday Service. Father James cultivates a sense of congregation, a collective coming together of likeminded people, whilst breaking down traditional perceptions of what a parish must be.

-- **Louise Tebbutt,** *Executive General Manager Human Resources, Risk and Safety Myer*

This book challenges every church to find ways to adapt and change in the 21st century. The work is large in scope and many of the ideas will be confronting for those who see their church as a comfortable and stable old friend. Yet it would be wrong to say that Father James proposes all past practices should be discarded or that the teachings of the Catholic Church should deviate from conservative belief. Rather the work recognises the importance of the church's history, tradition and place in the community but seeks to make these foundations relevant for the modern worshipper. Father James suggests a clear way forward for church leaders and parishioners – ask what can I do to keep my church meaningful in today's world? The book gives hope that the Catholic Church will remain a place of faith and succour for the remainder of this century.

-- **Peter Clarke**, *Melbourne Lawyer*

Fr James Grant manages to re-energise Catholic priests in our day and age when we feel more like closing down the shop. With his optimistic outlook and pastoral experience, he gives us many clues about how to tackle the challenges of our 21st century. He doesn't shy away from the obstacles of a modern day parish and shows us the way forward: innovate or die.

Knowing him, I had the pleasure to read his book and find the topics we discuss from time to time: these things are in his mind and he tries to give some answers. He doesn't have time for blaming the past or looking to the dark clouds of the future. He lives in the present time, tries to be objective and offer us priests, many different ideas to put into practice straight away. Polemics or debates don't bog him down; he manages to be practical and go down to basics. We should be grateful for his effort.

-- **Fr Joseph Pich**, *Opus Dei Community Melbourne*

Adherence to the past, whether an ideally-imagine past or an actual one, can in this highly competitive landscape, almost guarantee a steady slide into obscurity and irrelevance.

Let There Be Light is a read that pulls no punches; it kicks open the doors and loudly heralds a call for change. We need but to stand back a moment, open our eyes, and it becomes very clear that change is exactly what is needed.

For thousands of years, the social fabric of the world changed very little; but that is no longer the world we inhabit. Adaptation is now the key to survival and growth, for any organization; the church being no exception.

This book suggests a severance of old ties to outdated parish cliques and past glories; and proposes a powerfully outlined transition toward a modern model of the role that the church might play into today's society.

Even though this book may challenge some old and entrenched ideas, its real purpose is to illuminate, inspire and encourage others to step up and embrace an ethos of leadership that will pave the way for a better world tomorrow.

-- *John Will*, *Australia's Leading Martial Arts Instructor*

Drawing on his extensive overseas and Australian experience of parish life, Father James Grant shows that, despite rising secularism and religious apathy in the West, there is no need for priests and parishioners to accept an inevitable decline in parish life and activity.

His key insight is that churches have to move with the time while staying true to their core beliefs. This does not mean reading the zeitgeist of passing fashions or pursuing political causes from the pulpit. Many traditional faith brands such as Methodism and Presbyterianism have virtually disappeared, while erstwhile pillars of yesteryear, such as the Anglican Church, are rapidly withering on the vine. By trying to blend political causes with religious beliefs they have only succeeded in confusing their lifetime supporters, while failing to persuade activists to come on board. Activists may be passionate about their pet causes, but they don't need to do so within a church framework.

The Catholic Church has over a billion adherents worldwide and is still expanding in many countries – not because it bends with the political wind but because it stays true to its long held beliefs. Even those who don't strictly follow its teachings on such subjects as contraception and divorce can still admire its consistency of purpose and high principles. After all, its basic message of primacy for the poor and disadvantaged is a timeless and peerless one, which first captured hearts and minds nearly two thousand years ago.

The bulwark of modern society has always been the family and family values, but what has previously been taken for granted is now under vigorous assault. Marriage is becoming an optional extra for many, while its definition is undergoing profound re-thinking. But a multitude of studies have shown that those who have settled family lives are much more likely to achieve both material and spiritual prosperity, as well as a greater degree of happiness and life satisfaction.

Father Grant gives many practical examples of what a forward thinking but traditional values based programme can achieve. Those who already attend church are almost, by definition, amenable to an offer of further spiritual uplift and would be willing to contribute to community and parish life in various ways, if they can see an active agenda. Those who have turned away or are still looking for something to fill the spiritual hunger gap would be attracted by a parish priest and council which is keen to engage them on issues of mutual concern, whether pastoral or charitable. Care and compassion and concern for the poor should be core business for churches. So a programme which marries the traditional values and teaching of the gospel with the busy lives of ordinary people should have widespread appeal. Father Grant shows that this can, indeed must, be done if the Catholic Church is to remain vibrant and relevant to the lives of ordinary Australians.

-- **Richard Alston**, *former barrister who from 1986 to 2014 was a Liberal Member of the Australian Senate. From 1996-2003 he was Minister for Communications and the Arts and Deputy Leader of the Government in the Senate. From 2005-2008 he was Australian High Commissioner to the United Kingdom in London.*

CONTENTS

1. CONTINUOUS ADAPTATION – A MODERN REALITY	13
2. KNOW YOUR TURF	21
3. KNOW YOUR ENEMIES	26
4. IT'S ABOUT YOU OR IT'S ABOUT THEM	33
5. THE BUCKET	39
6. THE PIPELINE	45
7. DEMOGRAPHICS - WHERE ARE THE YOUNG?	51
8. ACHIEVING EARLY WINS	57
9. VOCATION AND MISSION	63
10. THE PAST IS NOT A PARADISE	75
11. MEMBERSHIP AND PARTICIPATION	83
12. PARISH LEADERSHIP	89
13. THE INVISIBLE PARISH	95
14. IDENTIFY AND ENERGIZE YOUR LEADERS	103
15. EXCELLENCE RULES	109
16. CATHOLICS ARE DOERS WHO REVIEW THEIR RESULTS	117
17. SETBACKS ARE NORMAL: BUILDING RESILIENCE	123
18. ONE SIZE DOESN'T FIT ALL: DIVERSITY THE BEGINNING OF GROWTH	131
19. THE GLOBAL PARISH	
20. WORK, FAMILY AND CATHOLICISM: WHAT REALLY DRIVES YOUR PARISH	137
ABOUT THE AUTHOR	145

1
Continuous Adaptation: A Modern Reality

The modern world has a number of important characteristics, prominently amongst them is the fact that change will happen to you, even if you yourself do nothing to bring it about. All individuals and organisations that fail to continually adapt are at risk of decline, irrelevance, takeover, financial stress and ultimately extinction. It is the central trait of flexibility and adaptation that is intimately related to growth, prosperity and the birth of new understanding.

The disquieting reality for many priests and parishes is that they have long stopped accepting this reality, or failed to consider its vital importance to effective ministry and parish mission.

Here then is a crucial idea, if you want a more vibrant parish with increased numbers, then you will need to change and adapt. If you are unable to cope with this reality, *that you must change*, then stop reading now. No amount of cajoling, arguments, new parish programs or mission statements have any hope of building on an attitude that is surreptitiously anti-change.

Truthfulness, about the reality of your own life or your parish community is hard to do, so difficult in fact, that most fail to even consider such questions. Overwhelmingly, the "average" person and the average parish has reached a "comfort zone" position where contentment, the quiet life and an aversion to conflict have taken precedence.

From personal experience I can highlight many parishes that talk about mission, attracting new members and gaining more youth, yet are unwilling to change parish bulletins, consider new signage or even a change in service times. These parishes are not serious about new growth or concepts of resurrection and resurgence.

At the core and starting point of all discussions about change must be a firm understanding of where you and your parish are currently positioned.

In broad terms there are two stark choices:

> Firstly, you are a *Church*. You cater for a wide range of differing individuals and ethnic groups, your programs, services and other offerings show a good balance between younger people, middle aged and the elderly. Your ministry team is varied with differing specialities. You operate a number of events that allow newcomers to participate fully. You strongly encourage family participation in as many parish events as possible. You provide some charitable services to your local areas. You have local instructional programs highlighting differing aspects of the faith and your local reputation in your area is respected.
>
> Or secondly, you are a *club*. You have been witnessing steady decline for a number of years and you have trouble attracting and holding new members. Your core worship group contains a solid group of parishioners who have attended loyally for many years but are now ageing. You have inconsequential youth or children's ministries, you are charitable and generous, yet this does not seem to attract others. You are not well known in your community, you have a view that things do need to change, but that such decisions reside with the priest. You consider yourself friendly, yet this affection is directed at existing members not newcomers. You generally lack energy and do little to contact with the wider community. You have not changed your notice sheets, signage or service times for years.

In the Western context the truth is that what we currently call a parish or a Church is no such thing. We are mostly clubs engaged in the management of decline. Until we are prepared to accept such realities, we will not be capable of the examination and interpretations needed for new growth.

Bottom Up Innovation

One of the most difficult concepts for leadership groups to embrace is that you are not the fount of all wisdom. Indeed, successful leadership groups understand themselves with almost the exact opposite perception.

The most important insight you bring to the oversight and direction of your parish is the recognition that your people know more than you know and that you need to ask them to contribute ideas, guidance, perceptions and concrete suggestions towards future growth and actions. This may sound the most obvious of positions, yet it is one that is hardly ever attempted. Many parishes have never asked their people for any input at all, in the future direction of their community life. Indeed, this may be such an unusual circumstance that some parishioners may see this as an abrogation of your responsibility. Encouraging your people to make suggestions, talk about future possibilities and be courageous enough to face difficult circumstances (especially the failures) will always take more than one conversation. A fundamental sign that a leadership group is functioning well is that it checks and rechecks its direction and goals. This means returning to your people on a regular basis. Naturally, the great barrier to such an attitude is the comfort of "set and forget", making one change, getting agreement from your people and then forgetting them again. This changes nothing as it does not re-enforce the message that you want your parish to learn, that you will make mistakes and that you will check with the people who matter: Your people.

Whilst the Church is not a democracy and priests and leadership groups are charged with decision making, to ignore your most important asset ensures that you will encounter passive and active resistance or more seriously just plain indifference. In the modern world people vote with their feet, loyalty must be earned and whilst your parishioners may not leave and go elsewhere they are highly likely to become passionless and attend only for reasons of duty showing no inclination to contribute to community growth. Such a reality is unfortunately common in many of our parishes: extinction awaits.

Learn what to look for

The most common response from parishes that are not oriented towards continuous adaptation will be, "what do you want us to do"? How can we help do what you want? These are absolutely the wrong responses. The elementary and paramount question must always be what do you (the people) want to do? What are the people's aims and objectives for their parish?

At the beginning of such a process the answer almost certainly will be "we don't know? What do you mean? And perhaps a desire to return to the idea that the leadership group should articulate more strongly what it wants to achieve.

The hardest job in developing parish thinking about continuous adaptation will be "getting people to begin to think for themselves" For such a process to become normal, the leadership team will need to consider a number of sessions helping groups to begin this idea of thinking about themselves and the possibilities that may exist in the future.

Importantly, this starts with the gaps:

- What do we not do in the parish?
- What must we be doing to be considered a full parish?
- What gaps in our offering can we fill tomorrow?
- What niche/unusual ideas could be considered that will give us a purpose?

These are the sorts of questions that are necessary when considering a changed future, particularly for people who are not used to moving anywhere!

The ability to look for gaps or niche markets is the most important skill you can teach your parishioners. It does a number of important things. Firstly, it suggests to parishioners that they can see and claim their own future, they are not dependent on intelligent or purposeful outsiders to do the work for them. Secondly, it means that your thinking develops in local ways: here is an opportunity for us now, in our areas, without competition, in which we can provide something useful to our community and finally it builds confidence that God's intention for us is to thrive, not just maintain things that have always been done. Certainly, all Catholic parishes will always be focused around the Eucharistic table, that is unchangeable, but what are the things that pull people into this greater commitment? What programs do we have that introduce us to newcomers in our areas? What do we do to teach others about us? What ways do we express the commitment of our weekend masses to those who don't know of our existence?

Learning from experience

Learning from experience is an essential aspect of continuous adaptation. In my view most parishes are clearly aware of what doesn't work, often because it is easiest to see. The youth group that never changes its size or the family services which continues to be based around one or two families are usually clearly visible. It is important to understand these negative experiences on a number of different levels: leadership, location, timing, resources and the individuals involved.

Foremost, don't keep doing the same things and expect things to get better. The Holy Spirit calls us to change and adapt. If leadership of a struggling youth group is shallow, then it becomes important for a parish to move to add stronger leadership. It may not be necessary in most cases to close groups or programs for the sake of it, but it will be necessary to understand a theological model of adaptation. God calls each parish to mission. An attitude that suggests things can't be done or shouldn't be done is fundamentally anti-mission. Not to try things, is a lack of faith in the workings of the Holy Spirit.

Judging what is working, especially in its initial phases, is much more difficult. This is usually as things are messier at the outset of new programs, results are hard to see, and planning may evolve in ways not necessarily seen at commencement. New programs need to be given time. Be prepared to let new development go in ways not foreseen, but start with fixing what you know not to be working.

Go Deeper

Adapting to change requires that you can understand the subtexts of things that you commence. At the outset of a new group or program, it's often the case that new alleys or pathways can be visualised. I am a firm believer in tracking, analysing and pursuing where these journeys may lead. They are not to be ignored, they are part of the flavour of what God gives to each parish, they may actually lead to a rich vein of mission and passion. Nevertheless, you must still give your primary reason for the establishment of a group time to mature and grow. An example of this kind of structure may surround a youth group with a solid core of 15-20 under 20's. But let's imagine 6 of that group decide they have a common love of music and wish to begin meeting together to sing or play. Would you stop this because it may fracture the larger group? A much more reasonable approach is to keep the larger group together, but allow the six to attract others from outside who may also love singing and playing instruments. Sub-groups are not harmful, provided they are managed, encouraged in their particular strength but also made available to the wider youth group and larger parish networks.

Harness complaints, whingers and crazies

Every parish has a healthy number of protesters, grumblers and those who are prone to fault finding. This is unfortunately part of the human condition and it is sad for those who have entered a world where that's all they do. It will be necessary to dedicate some form of outlet for these people to be heard. My suggestion is always to encourage people to put complaints into written form. Individuals who do not have the courage of their convictions by committing a complaint in writing and signing it should not be heard. This is one way to encourage the wider parish to ignore whinging and gossip by publically insisting that genuine complaints will obtain a reasoned response, if they take the time to email or write. The parish should be trained to understand that anything less than this is just destructive gossip to be rejected with vigour.

It is important that you continue to tell your wider parish the way you intend to do business. This needs constant reinforcement: We are a parish that is continuously adapting – this is not failure – this is our method for strengthening our structures, attracting new people, growing our parish in a variety of ways and fulfilling God's call to mission. Not only do we pray unceasingly, we do mission unceasingly.

Many people find new parish beginnings uncomfortable, particularly at the outset. Not all parishioners will be able to relate to the parish leadership team and some will prefer the old ways of life within the familiar: change is not easy. Yet the state of many of our parishes demands greater adaptability and a renewed determination to place mission at the forefront of what we do.

CONTINUOUS ADAPTATION: SYNOPSIS

- Change is perpetual: if your parish fails to adapt or reform you are at serious risk of decline.
- Many parishes are locked into "comfort zones" and are not serious about new growth and resurrection.
- Parishes have choices to transform into "Churches" or Clubs".
- Successful innovation comes primarily from parishioners.
- Successful leadership checks and rechecks direction and goals with parishioners.
- "Niche" ideas and "gaps" in community offerings give vision and purpose for ways to grow your parish.
- Parishes must "claim" new futures, not just accept leadership proposals.
- The things you do badly often point to a clear future.
- Be prepared to follow diversions to see where they lead.
- Be prepared to harness dissenters.
- Continuous adaptation is not failure but a method of strengthening your structures and attracting new people.

2

KNOW YOUR TURF

It may seem an amazing claim, but most priests and most parishioners don't actually know their local areas very well. Essentially you must treat your parish as a *sphere of influence*. This is the place where you do your work and if you don't know the area, then it will not be possible to do any serious work. This is a reality that is regularly overlooked by too many parishes. Mistakenly, some parishes believe an in-depth knowledge of the area is purely physical: our parish has 3 supermarkets, 2 pubs, 4 doctors, 1 chiropractor etc., what else are we supposed to know?

Well, let's start with demographics, how many people live in your parish? What is their make up? (How many families, singles, elderly, teenagers) How many work and where do they work? Is this parish one that is a dormitory parish for somewhere else? What is the average length of stay in your parish? The average income stream? If there are adolescents in the parish, where do they work, study or go to university? How many of the families in your parish are double income? If you don't know these statistical things regarding demographics, then you are already flying blind – and you are already at a severe disadvantage in forming community connections.

Nevertheless, of much more importance is your knowledge of more personal and cultural details. Does your parish area have an historical story or cultural formation? Did the original people in your area come for a particular reason, were they farmers, market-gardeners, fisherman, gold miners? These stories are important to know and understand even if there is no "original" activity that currently takes place. Why? Because they offer a parish the possibility of connecting into or developing a community myth.

Secondly, the history of your own Catholic community is important. Why did the parish originally commence? What was its connection to the local area? Was it established to serve a particular need? What were the first priests like? Did they have a particular charism or work orientation? The foundation of your parish, its organisation and the nature of your first priests gives an important guide to the DNA of the Parish. Most likely much of this information will be lost, yet pointers to the original expression of your parish also allow another significant dimension to be added: It shows your original and intimate connection to the area, it allows you to highlight, and emphasis a significant past and it encourages the current parishioners that they stand in a tradition of service, worship and connection to the area that extends beyond themselves.

It is therefore vitally important that old photographs, construction plans, photo of past priests, records of services, be displayed in a prominent location within your Church buildings. Such display, expresses clearly that difficulties were overcome, resilience was shown, loving and long serving devotion was achieved. In short, the fact that you exist, is a model of success, and in the face of current troubles or turbulence it states clearly that you have survived with certain traits in evidence and that you will survive and thrive again. If you have not already done so, commission a history of the parish to be written, but importantly one that continues into the present day. Parishes that are struggling to attract and hold new members are almost always missing a past. When you enter a sporting club, you will always see memorabilia of past champion teams, premiership cups, photos of significant players: Why? Because it bonds the present and the future into a tradition that has worked: and will work again! It also injects a sense of pride into the club. This brings us to the difficult issue regarding parishes whose past was perhaps less than best, particularly those that have suffered at the hands of abusive or paedophile priests. Let me say outright, there is no point ignoring this past or denying this, even though many years may have passed, there will still be significant numbers of people within the wider geographic community who will remember, harbour hostility, or be actively looking for opportunities to highlight your past failings.

In a number of parishes, paedophile priests will have caused significant local damage or indeed being responsible for family destruction, life failures, marriage break-ups or even suicide. Whenever something goes wrong in your parish this will be remembered and highlighted even if comments do not come to your ears directly.

Honesty is essential, it is important to acknowledge and even note in the parish history that these events have happened. Such a position allows a parish to do a number of creative things.

Firstly, it shows that you are aware of your own shortcomings, but most importantly it allows you to highlight proudly what you have achieved since. Yes, we have had instances of serious failure in the past, but we have made amendments, and because of recognition of our failures we have been able to achieve so many things that are new and beneficial – Here the message is slightly different, we are a learning community and because we can learn, heal and forgive, we are consequently creative and renewing, therefore new life is possible from failure and we have a story that confirms this. This is actually a story of even more good news than one where a parish has no significant black marks. Fragile human beings make mistakes, we are an example of how to overcome and rebuild.

Nevertheless, none of these reasons are the central reason for knowing your parish turf. Most importantly all viable parishes must be able to identify and sustain *areas of influence*. This is the place where you seek to influence a debate, commence targeted programs, and highlight to your wider community, essential and specific ways you make a difference to your area. If for example, your understanding of your local community leads you to conclude that "youth" services or "youth recreation" areas are under-sourced, you have identified a need that you potentially have an opportunity to fill. At this stage it is not about being put off by a lack of resources or financial constraints, but it is actually about identifying and being energised by a potential area of influence. Very few parishes are conscious of a community area of influence. Let me state the obvious, *if you have no area of influence within your wider community, then you do not rate in that community*! Despite your history, good intentions or fabulous buildings, you will be non-players in your area, relevance, significance and community credit come from what you do, not from just being. Naturally, for Catholics, the sacramental life and attending mass are at the core of who we are, nevertheless, parishes that only highlight mass times, risk being viewed as a "specific" club by outsiders. We know that mass is the most important thing we do, yet we must always be careful that we are just talking to ourselves, and centrally we must give outsiders significant opportunities to see us in a number of different ways. People join parishes because they can identify common links to their own lives, values and hopes. If a parish does little in this area, they make it far too easy to keep driving past!

Importantly, this is what an area of influence gives a parish, contact with the wider community beyond their own internal workings and a major opportunity to increase awareness to others about your value and the centrality of the mass.

There are a number of important considerations in identifying, promoting and beginning to project into an "area of influence". Firstly it is preferable that the area is not shared by others. If you start a youth group at your parish that is the fourth in the district, then it will certainly be harder to distinguish your particular offering from others. If you intend to enter a reasonably filled space, then vitally, the uniqueness of what you offer must be highlighted. Don't just do things to be run of the mill, they must be substantially different, better run, with a high degree of excellence. Copies of existing programs, without a markedly "catholic" flavour are destined to fail.

Secondly, your initiatives must also be specific and practical. Too much of what parishes do is lacking in practical application. Each parishioner should be able to promote your "area of influence" by being familiar with the work. That means, practical outcomes, "our youth group has 30 kids, concentrates on the children of single mums and meets Monday and Thursdays for 2 hours". An average parishioner who is able to parrot these details is a walking and talking billboard for your work, but most importantly demonstrates ownership of a program, pride in the initiative, and a practical aspect to "Catholic life". Catholic parishes that do not "do" stuff, that is practical, easily demonstrated and talked about will struggle to connect and can hardly complain that no new people join their community.

KNOW YOUR TURF: SYNOPSIS

- If you do not know your area you cannot do serious work within it.
- Demographics are important but cultural and historical knowledge is vital.
- Your parish "history" must be "known" and "acclaimed" – it provides examples of resilience, devotion and achievement.
- Parishes that "struggle" are missing a past.
- Parishes with "dark histories" need honesty and thoughtfulness for transforming these events.
- Parishes must be able to "identify and sustain areas of influence (where you target and highlight your work).
- Parishes without an area of influence do not rate in their community.
- Parish programs within an area of influence should not copy the programs of others.
- Programs that work are mostly practical.

3

KNOW YOUR ENEMIES

It should not come as a surprise to acknowledge that hostility to Church initiatives is widespread in some areas of the community. If you are not aware of this, or somehow doubt this as a reality then you as a parish are not living in the real world. In recent years the Church, particularly under the leadership of Pope John Paul II and Pope Benedict XVI, has come to recognise that the Church in essence is counter-cultural. Pope John Paul II often referred to a modern Church living within a "culture of death". Whilst this term highlights destructive practices of human life, including abortion, euthanasia, embryonic cell research, suicide, cloning and human sterilisation, the counter-culture nature of Catholic life can also be seen clearly in its ongoing promotion of matrimony, fatherhood, fidelity in marriage and family values.

The wider Church and local parishes do now encounter a higher number of individuals and community groups with values and practices that are fundamentally promoting practices we might consider as anti-Catholic.

This does not mean that a local parish is required to "confront" its enemies on a daily basis, or even organise events against them (that process is almost always counter-productive) but it must understand their viewpoints and have concrete reasons why Catholics disagree. From time to time local government councils do financially support and encourage groups that seem to promote an anti-Catholic bias. I have strong recollections of gay and lesbian mardi gras being permitted to parade past Churches during mass on Sundays. Responsible individuals on all sides of a debate are needed to ensure that altercations do not occur. It is nevertheless important to know why you oppose such activities and who to turn to for effective support.

"Australian marriage equality supporters" have sought to restrict Catholic material on marriage being promoted within Catholic schools, suggesting that these practices are discriminatory. Such organisations actively seek to silence religious voices and to erode Catholic beliefs on equality and discrimination. It is no longer acceptable to be unaware of such tactics or to suggest they are unfair. The world has changed, hostility to Catholics has increased, effective argument from a Catholic perspective needs to be in readiness. In 2015, St James Brighton, Victoria was destroyed by fire, one notable local celebrity suggested such events were "cathartic" for the wider community (given the alleged activities of a paedophile priest in the 1990's). No Church spokesman or lay Catholic was to be heard on radio or TV to rectify such uninformed views. If we are unable to bat for our beliefs, particularly at local level, then we allow such outrageous views to take hold in community thoughts and attitudes. Within any community there will be a number of organisations who might be considered natural supporters of Church activity. Local service clubs are a good example, their orientation towards helping and building local initiatives often sees a philosophical similarity to the Church. These groups present an opportunity to cement relationships and indeed to undertake partnerships, even if such partnerships remain primarily on a social level. We should not underestimate the importance of shared goals and values or the ability to work together over a problem or a future project. Shared understandings which lead to trust are a key way that "Catholic values" and ideas can be shared with others in ways that are not conflict driven.

On a deeper level community partnerships also bring with them critical levels of understanding, knowledge and insight into local problems along with insight into how best to pursue your community goals. There is no substitute for local knowledge and appropriate relationships with community leaders prepared to help.

At this point, clear sighted parishes will recognise the need to establish a local body of partners which may meet regularly to pursue common goals or to provide expertise to parishes over local needs, resources, people with leadership and appropriate knowledge. This "body of experts" is important for a number of reasons. Firstly, it will ensure a constant source of new ideas, new local people and potential future projects. Secondly, it will ensure that your parish is seen as a key local contributor and play-maker in the region. In the end, a parish will be required to do its own work towards its own projects. This should not be a body to whom you outsource Catholic "things", but rather a group of active-supporters and minor partners who support your fundamental goals. Success will be easier with strong locals who "get" what you are on about.

Perhaps the most difficult form of enemy is the internal one. These can often be small groups of parishioners who do not "like the priest", may resist change, or don't see any value in community engagement. It is perfectly reasonable for a parish council to identify such people, it is not reasonable to demonise or bully them. Within a successful parish the nature and scope of community involvement, pastoral activities, liturgical functions, youth and family ministries and administration should provide a vast array of potential alternatives for disaffected individuals to get their teeth into. Ignoring people and hoping they will go away doesn't work, for the individual, or the parish. In all successful parishes, the sometimes highlighted, but mostly unstated goal is that all parishioners "do" something. What you do may be left to an individual but in the modern parish (which needs to function) all parishioners must be working towards a supported parish goal. We Catholics, talk incessantly about mission, evangelisation and building parish community. In reality, we do very little of it. All baptised parishioners know this in their hearts, but very often don't have the necessary parish goals, incentives or encouragement to activate a viable functioning ministry.

The other great enemy within a parish is simply lack of energy and internal indifference. Many modern parishes are plagued with this reality, but simply choose to ignore it. Somehow, someday, something will change: the sermons will get better, the musicians will finally gel.

Parishioners will arrive on time and not leave early, the microphone batteries will not fail and the building might be sufficiently heated and lit. Of course, nothing will change unless parishioners themselves are prepared to no longer accept an attitude of indifference, exhaustion and near enough is good enough. If an attitude of excellence does not pervade your parish, then long-term growth will not be possible. The parish that produces mediocrity is only viewing its life as one of maintenance.

One day an energetic priest will arrive, some young people will appear and even some families might come for more than confirmation!

These are all the attitudes of a dying parish. They must be vigorously crushed, constantly challenged and named for what they are: the language of people without vision.

Consequently, the parish council must contain a significant proportion of individuals who have bought into the energetic parish vision of the future. It is no longer good enough to issue notices as if they don't concern each person or they only refer to Wednesday's prayer group. Any announcement that suggests we need you to "do your duty" and attend this function to help with this school event should go to the bottom of the pile. The key and perhaps only function of notices, parish bulletins, headmaster's School Reports or any other communication is to reinforce, highlight and excite others about the parish vision. The underlying message must always be, we are a successful, energetic, up and running parish because we do such and such. If you are not always talking about the excitement of your programs and vision, then you are not building them, you are killing them through boredom. The attitude of the parish leadership group must always be one of energy, excitement and a bright spirit filled future. Importantly, those who speak to the parish in any capacity need a small amount of training, so that articulation of the parish goals and who we are as a people, never gets lost in boring communication. Each year the average parish confirms around 40-50 teenagers who attend with their usually "duty bound" parents, very few of these people are ever seen at mass again. Nevertheless they do have some level of commitment and responsibility, it's also the case that most parishes bore them senseless with internal matters which subconsciously tell them that they don't belong amongst you. Energy, vision and future is all they should see, lifeless, indifference must be a thing of the past.

KNOW YOUR ENEMIES: SYNOPSIS

- The parish in the modern world is counter-cultural.
- The modern parish must understand the argument of opponents and have a firm grasp of Catholic counter views.
- Parishes must establish relationships with like-minded community groups.
- Internal enemies must be creatively directed to support parish goals.
- Parishes which concentrate on excellence grow. Those that produce mediocrity decline.
- All parish communications must be energetic and highlight success. Negative or boring individuals should not speak on behalf of the parish.

4

It's about you or It's about them

Growing and expanding your parish requires brutal honesty so let's start with the ruthless truth. Virtually every parish action, function, liturgy, meeting, sermon, or group in your parish is about *You*. That's right, your needs, your desires, your hopes, your aims, your people, your building, your priest – these are the things that take precedence in your parish community.

How do I know this, because every parish talks and talks about mission, yet invariably delivers little. Many parishes that do start something stop after a few months, often resigned to the idea that "it can't be one" or "it can't be done now – maybe in a year or two" and many parishes that start mission point to those who objected to the new idea and decided to leave. That's right, a strongly developed missions focus will *cost* you, often some people you might feel you cannot afford to lose.

Let's be ruthless again – *mission means change and change means cost* and here is the central reason why it is very rarely started or sustained, *we are afraid of the consequences and the real possibility that we will go backwards before we move forward.*

Parishes have usually developed a whole range of language and thinking that makes change difficult, locks people into the past, and suggests that preservation is the highest good.

I am a natural conservative; probably most Catholics are, after all we believe we have a great "thing" that is worth spreading and preserving: why invent the wheel again, the faith works for me as it is, shouldn't it work for everyone?

The language of preservation is everywhere "The Church has been here for two thousand years, it will be here for another two thousand. "Our Church is the historic centre of our town, there would be no town without us, or 'Christianity is the foundation of the western world', without the faith there would be no democracy, no women's' rights no freedom of the individual etc. etc."

All of these statements are true, but they elicit a truth that is locked into a past and invertedly suggests that the present or the future has its value only from the foundations that have been laid.

And more shockingly, nobody actually thinks this anymore, especially if they are under 35 years of age. When you use this language you are speaking a dead language. This language also puts an emphasis on the Church as institution not on the Church as people; if we've been here for two thousand years, why worry, we will always be around. This language saps energy, results in lethargy and risks creating a false sense of internal superiority. Jesus won't abandon us so we don't have to do much. Of course, the reality throughout the world is different, the Church has vanished from large parts of the world or been crippled into virtual non-existence. The vibrant Middle East and Anatolian Christianity is long gone, along with the faith in North Africa and in the last decade much of Syria and Iraq. Naturally, the Church will change and adapt, but let's not imagine that western Christianity is immune from extinction, the rise of secularism and the huge growth in Islam in western nations requires a need to think again regarding unvarying and continuous existence.

All Church communication must be wary of any language, or ideas that support the lazy thought that the Church will always go on, as if the institution is somehow not dependent on people. It is people who matter, not only their private faith, but their ability to engage, connect, attract and speak to their local community. Any language, mission statements, or sermons that suggest a "new normal" of a small diminished, more faithful church is indolent. These are excuses for not understanding or undertaking mission. They should be rejected for the faithlessness they contain.

Therefore, the Church's mission is not about you, accordingly it's about "them"! This is a difficult psychological space in which to exist, but it is the only place that allows authentic mission to form and to expand. Your constant parish questions, language, goals and hopes must be about "them", i.e. every person in your district who is not currently part of your parish. Therefore, you must know and understand these people. Who are those in your parish that need your help? Who sends their kids to your schools? Who are the individuals suffering loss, bereavement or change? Who is looking for community? Who is without family in the area? There are gaps in every community which call for a church response. It does not mean every niche market will gravitate to your services, but it must mean above all that you are aware of these sub-communities, that you speak their language and that your words and actions suggest openness and partnership to them. Before you can do something for your community you must know who *they* are, that's the first item, the sad truth is that most parishes haven't got a clue about "them"

Changing your parish culture to reflect new priorities is always difficult. A necessary first step must be formation of an enthusiastic group of laity who can see the value of community engagement. The role of the priest is important for encouragement and leadership, but no individual can be aware of all that has formed or developed within your parish boundaries. New individuals and communities enter a parish all the time. A wide group of parish people must be aware of such movements and have the necessary skills to engage with them. Leadership, in this instance must be focused on sustaining the energy and ability to think outside the box that this group of people must have. In many ways, this group must be risk takers, individuals who are resilient and prepared for rejection. Authentic engagement with your community means you will regularly encounter a wide variety of community indifference, laziness and sometimes open hostility. Mostly you will encounter amazement and surprise. Why is the Church seeking to engage with us? What do they want? Can they be trusted? Importantly, the reasons for engagement with particular community groups need to be thought through. If, for example, you seek engagement with local groups only to raid their databases, you will find rejection is the most common response. If however you propose an innovative way of engaging with a joint community issue, you are likely to find a warmer reception. Creating these partnerships and links is vital to your parish future but, firstly you must know them. What are their core ideas, hopes, frustrations, failures and future projects and are they sufficiently in line with your own. When you have some idea of what these things look like, you may be able to engage in the beginning of authentic community partnerships.

This "outgoing community" individual is often hard to find within the regulars that attend your services. Why? Because usually your "rusted on" people, find it harder to see their need for change and mission and have already committed strongly to the "normal" offering of your Church. Consequently, it may be necessary, but also exciting and challenging to approach people who are "historically" less committed, or who have even stopped attending parish events. Individuals with a "light" commitment to your parish (but still a love for it) are often those with different or unusual ideas on how to engage local communities. It may be that these people can be both reactivated in their commitment to the "core" community and also bring a series of new approaches to community engagement and vibrancy to the central idea of mission beyond yourself. Most parishes have only a tiny circle of semi-committed people beyond their immediate parish. This is at the heart of our modern difficulties, for a parish in this situation has only a small pool of potential new parishioners. Sustained growth requires a substantial semi-committed grouping. Consequently, we can sum up the differences between a parish without much growth potential and one that has real expansion potential.

Parish A: Minimal growth potential

Large non-committed who know nothing of your beliefs, values & work

Small – semi-committed sub-group

Small – Central core

Parish B: Significant growth potential

Large non-committed who know nothing of your beliefs, values & work

Large – semi-committed sub-group

Small – Central core

In both these examples, the central core of dedication, loyal and committed parishioners is comparatively small. What is dramatically different is the size of the second layer, those who are semi-committed. The larger this group the greater the potential for growth and the stronger the changes for finding new leadership beyond your inner core. Because this group is naturally semi-committed they will need to be asked, cajoled and supported. People do not move into a committed state because they can see the obvious advantage of increasing their commitment, if they saw that they would already be part of the inner group. Importantly, they will need to be encouraged, valued, praised and educated on the value that they bring to the parish and wider community, but also the changes that have occurred within themselves. If we are not making better people and building modern saints, then parish core groups will be destined to remain small.

Finally, in our wider planning for growth, we also must consider a stronger projection into the domain of the uncommitted and those without knowledge of your parish. Naturally, this group is the layer that hopefully will provide a strong semi-committed core in future years. This requires a degree of promotional work and connectedness that may not show any advantage in the short term. Nevertheless, the lifting of parish awareness in the uncommitted space is not wasted.

In an increasingly secular world, Christians who support marriage, family, home buying and wider commitments in society may well be seen as strange. However, the counter-cultural nature of the Church has always been highlighted in our history. Rather, than risk misunderstanding, it is important for your parish to be seen for what it stands for. Our job is to open our community to the world not to be changed by it. This openness and integrity is our responsibility, parish growth remains God's!

IT'S ABOUT YOU OR IT'S ABOUT THEM: SYNOPSIS
- Most parishes are primarily concerned with themselves.
- Mission and parish growth are stifled by self-focus.
- Mission means change and change means cost, therefore some parishes are afraid to take risks.
- An obsessive concentration on preservation saps energy and initiative.
- Parishes that accept a "new normal" of reduced numbers and influence, degrade mission and encourage self-focus.
- Parish culture and goals must focus on outsiders and newcomers.
- Semi-committed individuals are the key to substantial growth.

5

THE BUCKET

When priests and parishioners talk about their hopes and vision for their parish, they often do so in terms of surplus, excess or over-abundance. Perhaps this harks back to the land of milk and honey, a place of natural fertility promised to the Israelites by God (Ezekiel 20.6).

Notwithstanding, the dubious reality of such visions, parishes that remember golden eras of "standing room only" have almost certainly glamorised the past, yet more critically conditioned future success on a vision of the past that is almost certainly wrong. All parishes are finite, in the sense of constraints related to the number of Catholics in an area, the physical size of school or parish buildings, the financial viability of the members and costs of keeping maintenance and future building aspirations within budgets.

A vision of endless overflowing abundance was never true in the past and will not be again in the future. Establishing future goals and vision must be related to achievable and sustainable growth, not wildly imagining unlimited growth blessed by God and then feeling unloved when such divine providence does not eventuate.

Naturally, parishioners will certainly have heard of stories relating to nearby "mega churches" who never fail to attract less than 5,000 people to their services each time. The problem with such comparison is the lack of understanding of what actually happens in these mega-church environments. Almost invariably the mega-church of 5,000 worshippers in 2005 is still the mega-church of 5,000 worshippers in 2015. The problem is they are not the same 5,000 people. Such churches are good at attracting new individuals, but not so good at holding them.

The truth of finite growth is still in operation for these Churches as well, with "newcomers" invariably cannibalised from other like-minded churches or from the vast pool of lapsed Catholics. The rise of huge evangelical churches in the United States and South America is largely based on appealing to former Catholics. They are not new Christians in the strict sense, but rather non-practising ones or those drawn to religious expressions associated with the Pentecostal and charismatic movements. The practice of Christianity in these mega-churches is often revivalist in style but is also distinctly ethnic. Two-thirds of Latino worshippers attend church with Latino clergy, Spanish based liturgy with largely Latino Christians in attendance. The Australian experience is not dissimilar with an apparent large appeal to Australians of Asian backgrounds (although English is the usual medium). Within the United States around 68% of Hispanics identify themselves as Roman Catholic; the next largest group around 15% are born again or converted evangelical Protestants. Almost all of these Evangelical Christians are former Roman Catholics.

Certainly, mega-evangelical churches have a solid record of attracting the lapsed Roman Catholic and those from minority ethnic groups who may feel "different" from the wider society. The evangelical emphasis on music and emotive preaching has two distinct aspects. It is usually neutral in its initial preaching and rather seeks to develop and sustain feelings of welcome, acceptance and belonging. Music is always of the same emotional character and is designed to highlight concepts of "conversion", the "grace of God" and the importance of the "personal relationship with Christ" as the consummate means of gaining acceptance, meaning, well-being and success.

To those of a Catholic background, the complete absence of sacramental life, the lack of Eucharistic centrality and abolition of devotion to Mary can seem to be shocking. Yet, for those Catholics with only a light touch in these central Catholic practices, barriers to understanding or a feeling that if I don't grasp the teachings I can't be part of the worship are not in play in evangelical churches. All that is required is the "feeling" that I belong and that others accept me.

Unexpectedly, these "seeds" of success for evangelicals are also the central reason for ultimate failure. Preaching based on emotion is certainly uplifting in its initial phases, but is difficult to sustain without messages of depth. In a similar manner, music without liturgical underpinning, only points to emotion and doesn't allow participants to particularly feel that progress is being made. Without a sacramental life pointing towards the fullness of Eucharist, most individuals will be unable to sustain Christian life. This phenomenon is strongly present in the life of mega-churches and results in a large number of disillusioned individuals leaving on a regular basis. The complication of such disappointment can result in the complete abandonment of the faith together.

It is important to apply alertness and comprehension to the certainty of human behaviour within parish communities (or for that matter, mega-churches). You may wish to be growing endlessly, but external or internal constraints will always ensure this cannot be maintained. Nevertheless, what can be achieved is more moderate growth, sustained over longer periods that will enable financial, staff and community growth to be applied through a number of generations. This is a significant achievement. As it currently stands, most Catholic parishes in Western nations are not achieving such outcomes.

Subsequently, it is critical for modern parishes to have in place a retention strategy. If we only concentrate on water coming into the top of the bucket, we may be unaware of the many holes at the bottom.

Most parishes are getting better at the friendly greeting and welcome team at the commencement of a Sunday mass, however, follow-up is still rather dismal. This role still often falls to the priest. It shouldn't. A regular new members visiting team should be charged with such responsibility. It is in meeting parishioners, learning where they live, what schools they send their children to, why they attend mass and what are their hopes for the future, that allows visitors to move from "outsider" to "insider" – this must be done as soon as practicable. Waiting to form these connections result in feelings of disinterest in newcomers. If I cannot make new connections with those who support and take interest in me, what will make me continue to return? Perhaps a good sermon or wonderful music, but most profoundly: human connection! A mass where a sizeable number of the congregation have left directly after communion or the final prayer speaks of duty and obligations (sometimes valid) but certainly not of substance and commitment.

It is an essential component of parish life to invite new members, their families and friends to particular parish functions that primarily allows trust to be established and grow. This does not need to be a burden but should come before calls to attended classes, teaching sessions or joining rosters and committees.

Parishes that display some talent at holding new parishioners are usually not doing so by chance. Perhaps inadvertently, they are doing a number of distinct activities that are designed to move "newcomers" to insiders as soon as possible. Parishes of this type often run "induction" gatherings, usually in an established members home, who assumes the responsibility of initial care for the new individual or family. It is here that meeting the priest or ministry team is done best. It is not overwhelming and it allows for convivial social interactions to develop. Learning about each other's journeys will not take place during mass celebrations, but may do so in these welcoming social environments. In the initial stages these are just as important as mass attendance and give the parish a chance to demonstrate your commitment to others. If you are constantly disappointed that newcomers cannot sustain mass attendance, you are focusing on their commitment to you. In the first instance the primary consideration should be your commitment to them.

Additionally, parishes with a strong focus on "newcomers" will usually direct these people into a mass that allows for more teaching or explorations as the liturgy moves through its various dimensions. These do not have to be "special services", but those parishioners who are helping the initial integration should be in attendance and the priests should be aware that formation may be taking place and adopt what they do in suitable ways. An important aspect is not overpowering the newcomer with endless information, but an appreciation of the beauty of the mass as it speaks to the human condition and as it speaks to their particular needs and hopes. In this instance a parish is seeking to impart care and concern for newcomers (as evangelistic churches do) but with a meaningful worship and teaching component. These two things go together; being loved and valued and worshipping honestly. Parishes that separate these aspects risk some newcomers feeling unwanted or others lost in comprehension regarding church teachings and practice. When any of these things happen you will lose people. The hole in the bucket outweighs the effort of filling.

An important consideration should be widespread in each parish that seeks to grow: We need to remember how hard it was when we first attended alone and knew no-one. Newcomers have shown real courage in walking through your door; it is not a case of diminishing that courage by lamenting their failure to return. That failure is yours, as you declined to recognise and reward their courageous move towards you. If you sit there and ignore them, or are not even aware of their presence, you are too focused on yourself and your own needs. Such an attitude will create a club not a Church.

I would consider the effort and courage to walk into a new environment, knowing nobody and not being sure of what awaits you as more resolute than bungy-jumping. In the same way such an achievement must be recognised and rewarded. If you do make your first bungy-jump, things are so much easier from there on in. Those who enter your building must be congratulated just for coming.

A word of warning must also be sounded on the way you present yourself to newcomers in your usual interactions between each other. Newcomers will very quickly identify those parishioners who are the "players", those who enjoy the favour of the priest, or those who appear to make decisions and have their say. It is also highly noticeable to newcomers those who are not "in" and those members without a voice. You may no longer see "cliques" with your parish, but it's the first thing "newcomers" will notice. Be warned, you must be aware of your own cliques, to weaken and destroy them. Cliques are a cancer within a parish, they destroy community life, leave members feeling abandoned and completely thwart any possibility of growth.

No parish can grow with cliques or factions. Why? Because you have shown newcomers your malady and disorders, who wants to join such a "diseased and unhealthy body".

The future for growth within the average parish is strong and full of potential, not least because this is God's intention for his church, nevertheless it remains our challenge to remove rotten or ailing dimensions to our community life and that again demands tenacious honesty.

THE BUCKET : SYNOPSIS

- Past Golden Eras are usually not based on fact.
- All parishes are finite but hard work can sustain improved numbers of parishioners.
- Parishes must have a retention strategy.
- Social interaction with newcomers highlights your commitment to them.
- It takes courage to enter a church building – newcomers need affirmation and praise.
- Newcomers to your parish will quickly identify cliques and favoured individuals, treating everyone equally is a must in attracting new people.

6

THE PIPELINE

In the Catholic world which highlights and emphasises lifelong commitment, one of the hardest facts to face is that this is no longer true, at least in the Western experience of the Parish. There is little statistical information available regarding commitment trends amongst Catholics, but parishes that contain large numbers of parishioners who have been attending mass for thirty years or more are fewer and fewer. In reality, a small handful of such individuals are likely. This in a sense is not problematic; it just means Catholic parishes must be more attuned to the certainty that comings and goings from parishes is quite normal. People move houses, districts, states and countries on a much more regular basis, chasing work, material benefits, marriage or fresh starts. In some Western nations the average parish will have completely cycled because of these desires to improve one's status, education or material gain within five years. A parish that contains such variability should not be seen as insecure or unsettled, yet does require new ways of thinking, particularly in relation to inconsistent growth.

In many parishes, notably rural ones, this fluctuation has always existed. Younger people will more to cities for education, work and marriage, accentuating the transient nature of some farming districts or towns whose initial reason for existence (mining, oil or plantation) may no longer be economically viable.

Death and resurrection is our central motif, nevertheless, this doesn't make such losses easier to take. With the rise of secular education and the loss of Catholic influence in the workplace, unions and the media, the task of keeping parishes at the forefront of people's minds is harder and will require more local effort.

Centrally, the task of mission and evangelism can never rest in the modern parish. We still see far too many parishes undertake mission weekends or mission months, and then do nothing for the remainder of the year. We also see far too many parishes promote one dimension of parish life, such as a traditional liturgy or unique choir as a central experience of the parish. To emphasise these dimensions exclusively is not mission. Mission is the extension, the stretching, the "plus" factor to *all* that the parish undertakes. Highlighting only one or two aspects of parish or community life is a receipt for disaster, is intellectually and spiritually lazy and shows no grasp of what mission is.

Underlying these concepts is a failure to understand the modern parish and more importantly the modern parishioner. It is no longer reasonable to expect parishioners, once engaged within your parish to remain with you for their whole Catholic life. Every parishioner has a shelf life. Every parishioner will have a finite time amidst your parish life and every parishioner that has entered the pipeline will ultimately depart from your midst.

It is failure to understand this new reality that makes so much of what is called mission completely ineffective.

Ineffective parishes and those that continue to complain about their inabilities to hold onto people have their focus on the wrong part of the pipe. Their aim and concentration is on maintaining what already exists, maintaining people within various roles, or maintaining a limited set of parish activities that are thought to be central to parish life. Here is a new contention: Concentration must be primarily on those who are just entering the pipeline and those who have only been engaged for a short period. These individuals are the future of the parish. All parishes will always be losing people for a variety of reasons - the important question is who is taking their place?

On the surface, this may sound unnecessarily ruthless, yet in my view each parish that is in decline operates in this way. There is not enough emphasis on "newcomers", lack of newcomers is the cause of decline, not the fact that people leave (that will happen anyway).

Parishes in decline devote too much, angst, energy and fear on maintaining a "core" number of people who are considered vital to survival. Sometimes, it may not actually be a particular individual, but a role, say a choir master, who must always be replaced, often at extreme financial cost. Parishes that concentrate on what cannot die usually ensure that it does. Concentrate and focus on the needs of newcomers and those entering your parish recently. They are the ones with the majority of their shelf-life still in front of them. Providing you understand this is the case, you will be able to effectively serve them and create more new entries. This is mission.

Naturally, individuals vary; priests and ministry teams are no different. Some priests are primarily skilled in maintaining and developing that which already exists. This is probably the majority. Another group of priests are driven to seek, encourage and develop the "newcomer", in my view a smaller cohort. Nevertheless, whatever the make-up of clergy or ministry teams; each parish must ensure that the central ministry focus is on developing the entry points for newcomers to successfully, engage and enter the parish. This requires significant thought and adaptation. It does not have to all depend on the priest but clearly defined roles and job descriptions must be accepted by a number of people within your parish who concentrate only and exclusively on the newcomers. Most modern parishes don't do this and are consequently in decline. This is the single biggest reason parishes fail to grow, nobody or no group is focused upon newcomers. This is a basic necessity and we can hardly complain about not attracting and holding newcomers when we are not prepared to focus intently upon them.

Psychologically, the departure of parishioners causes far too much angst and grief in struggling parishes. Once we accept this is normal, is going to happen, and may actually be beneficial to both the individual and the parish, we are beginning to think like a parish with a missionary orientation. Indeed the primary role of the missionary parish is to prepare others to go out, not to seek to keep them bound to your ways, models or thinking. Providing the sunshine and rain is God's business, ours is to cultivate and prepare the soil and nurture the growing buds.

It is of the utmost importance not to take the "natural given" of those leaving your parish personally. When a parish sees departure, as natural and normal, almost a moment of pride and success, then another valuable part of mission has been accomplished. A new part of God's action has developed in the world for use and mission elsewhere. Here is another important understanding for growing, mission orientated parishes: You are not preparing and developing people to keep them to yourself – in fact to do this is a fundamental failure. We develop and prepare individuals – parishioners, for work and mission in God's world, this may be in your backyard, but equally it may not. Parishes that wish to grow must keep their attention on those coming to and newly entering their pipeline. Anything that diverts your attention away from this is life threatening. Placing your attention on the correct end of the pipeline is the major key to growing a parish. New people are your lifeblood.

In some parishes, where worries about the future have increased, the taking of attendance records has developed; counting bums on seats usually only increases anxiety. Have you had a more successful year if your Christmas mass attendance has increased by 10, 15 or 20? What constitutes improvement? If you must keep statistics, do so on the ones that really matter, how many newcomers attend your parish this year. The truth is, few keep those statistics because they know what the results will be.

It is often said that some parishes or areas have an advantage over others. This is true; a new parish in an outer region with housing affordability will likely have greater opportunities to attract young families and children. This does not mean that an established inner-city parish without families has no future. It does mean that identification of areas of growth and potential new people needs to be more sophisticated. It may also mean the shocking reality that you may be called to attract and encourage individuals you may not have previously thought suitable or worthy of your parish. Such is life, your job is not to dislike or refuse to engage. It is to understand mission, it is to focus on those at the beginning, (or as yet without a beginning) and it is to widen the opening of your pipeline for all that God calls you to do.

THE PIPELINE: SYNOPSIS

- Individuals come and go from each parish: This is normal.
- Promoting only one or two areas of parish life is not mission and is intellectually and spiritually lazy.
- Each parishioner has a finite time within your parish life – A failure to understand this distorts mission objectives.
- Ineffective parishes are those who complain about their inability to hold parishioners – Their focus is on the wrong end of the Catholic journey.
- Successful parishes focus on those at the beginning of their parish life and designate skilled individuals to support them.
- Missionary parishes prepare individuals for their life beyond their parish.
- Missionary parishes do not prepare individuals to only keep them for themselves.
- Total attendance figures do not indicate the health of your parish, the number of newcomers does.

7

DEMOGRAPHICS – WHERE ARE THE YOUNG?

Most modern parishes have a striking demographic problem: they lack young people. In the Australian context the overwhelming majority of individuals who attend mass belong to the baby boomer category (50-70 years of age). Across the nation this grouping makes up around 26% of the population, in churches the percentage is around 50% or higher. There is only one conclusion that can be drawn from such a reality: Churches that exhibit these demographics are heading for extinction. The Catholic Church is not magically exempt from this impeding future, despite migrant flows from particular countries with devout Catholic population such as Vietnam, the Philippines and India. Changes and plans need to be put in place now to avoid a situation that will see average parishes placed increasingly in twinning (joining of parishes, sharing a priest) arrangements. The result of such compromises usually results in the management of slow decline, coupled with a psychology of maintenance ensuring that mission, outreach and community engagement are viewed as arduous and resource challenging. The truth for such parishes is exhausted clergy and key laity. What energy and initiative that does remain is focused on attempts to bring people into church buildings not on programs that offer something to others. The fundamental principle of all parishes must be "what do you do for your community? And how subsequently is your parish perceived in the wider area?" Do this well and you will have new membership. Concentration on drawing people into what already exists is bound to disappoint as it answers the wrong question "what do we need" "not what do we offer".

In general terms a number of other demographic groups are to be found in Western society, a generation X (34-49 years of age) making up around 20-25%, a generation Y (15-33 years of age) of around 25% and a generation Z (under 15 years of age) at around 15%. These groups are all psychologically different in attitudes to the modern world and importantly all different to the largest group that joins itself to parishes (the baby-boomers). Here is an obvious problem: the values, methods and hopes of those who attend mass are different from the crucial points and essence of the other groups. In many Australian parishes it is not difficult to see the absence of generation X, Y and Z. Yet, do we not somehow imagine that eventually all will be well and these groups will fall into line with the understandings of the baby boomers? There is no evidence to suggest that such a process has occurred in the last 30 years.

A significant 1991 study (Strauss and Howe "Generations") radically suggested that "generational types" seem to follow each other across historical periods. Naturally, there is much to be cautious about in such a view, yet it does give fruitful warning to parishes that we need to adapt our programs and focus our community life on the differing generations within our society. We should not need to be told this, yet our demographic reality means we need to learn fast.

In broad terms, baby boomers have been characterised as an idealistic generation with a strong social vision that was impatient to change the world, had a focus on humanity and were generally prepared to spend big, often with money they didn't have. This generation has focused on some big ticket human initiatives, universal health care, human-rights and the advancement of women's issues.

Perhaps, it is only natural that the generation to follow, generation X is much more circumspect, this generation has been predominantly concentrating on the environment, repairing economic damage and consolidating institutions and practices that benefit stability and order. Generation Y, seems much more concerned with wealth generation, pragmatic and rational solutions, but can sometimes be lacking in social concern. Generation Z are so far proving to be another socially aware generation, particularly on issues affecting the environment, they are proving to have strong leadership characteristics and tend to apply the gains from wealth creation to socially beneficial ideas. Whilst all of these "generations" are generalisations, they do point to an environment that the Church has generally neglected. Each generation is different in nature and requires different touch-points to attract and maintain its interests. A parish that fails to understand this will continue to decline whilst living in hope that something will miraculously change. Successful growth in parishes requires action and specific planning to attract and engage new people!

Many Catholic parishes also need to consider a few words of warning. World Youth day will do little to captivate or attach young people to your parish. You need local initiatives to do this. Whilst the vibe may energize some local youth to "discover" your parish, local programs will be absolutely necessary to maintain and grow newcomers in the faith.

It is also true that having a school attached to your parish is no guarantee that young people and their families will be seen in mass. Undoubtedly, the disconnection between the two institutions is proving in many cases a difficult gulf to overcome. Primary loyalty in these families is usually always to the school, self-interest demands this. Parishes may be seen as valuable add-on's, but few are usually viewed as little more than a dutiful additional burden. This is uncomfortable to admit, but a natural love of a parish community attached to the school is not a given. These connections can only be enhanced by specific programs "owned" and "organised" by the parish designed for these students. Attempts at coercing parents to bond to the parish "through" the school may be successful undertaken for short periods, but will not generate a significant loyalty to the parish in itself.

Attracting the students and parents of "your" school to "your" parish requires a whole new level of thinking, adaptation and commitment towards this cohort. Evidence strongly suggests they will not be "yours" through natural love or affection. This must be struggled for and built through hard work.

Accordingly, parishes who wish to engage with new people, especially those outside the baby boomer cohort need to adapt their structures and be prepared to make some decisive change.

Primarily, this will require installing a leadership group that has specific oversight towards the potential newcomers, but significantly this group must be within the age group themselves. If you want youth groups under 25 years of age, you require leadership from individuals the same age.

This does not mean allowing groups to do what they please. Reporting lines to parish priests and pastoral committees must be in place, nevertheless, the day to day face of these new groups must contain leadership developed, encouraged and supplied from their own. Youth Groups with baby-boomer leadership have short membership phases!

Training, encouraging and mentoring such new leadership is the role of the parish priest in conjunction with other wider parish leaders. Nevertheless, the nature of such groups requires trust and encouragement. Certainly, mistakes will be made but it is the parish priest's leadership role to ensure that these are avoided if possible by fully understanding the goals and intentions of the new groups.

In many cases it will be necessary to acquire leadership but perhaps not from traditional sources. This will require a parish priest and steering committee prepared to meet with outsiders, to build strong relationships and to effectively take over and immerse new leadership in Catholic ethos and tradition.

As the world becomes increasingly secular, it will be necessary to provide this "immersion experience" to all those who would work within your parish. It is likely many non-Catholics may be attracted to your vision for parish development. These individuals must be prepared to accept and operate within a "Catholic values structure" in the first instance. The process of encouraging these individuals to join your church is important. More central is creating an environment where leadership can be encouraged and formed that is, "essentially Catholic". Do this first, identify your leadership group, form, train and mentor them and get started! Do not wait for the perfect, fully prepared leader to stumble into your parish. This is not likely to happen and misunderstands the universal nature of Catholicism based on Christ's command to "go and make disciples of all nations" (John 23).

Such new leadership groups must be allowed to function and build a leadership framework that works for their "generation". This will mean allowing specific programs that others might not understand or be interested in. That's okay, not every parishioner wants to participate in every parish event. A group of little old ladies, who wish to help youth activities, need their enthusiasm directed into other activities. Unfortunately, sometimes these volunteers seem more interested in ensuring the failure of new initiatives, so be prepared to clear the decks of some "regular" helpers. New leaders will need their own space and a firm sense that they have the priest's support, the backing of the parish leaders and the confidence of the wider parish. Additionally, the building of social support and encouragement for the new leadership comes from positive advertising, good mentoring and a sense on both sides that newcomers are becoming "one of us", and on the other side that they are assured of welcome when they do!

DEMOGRAPHICS, WHERE ARE THE YOUNG?: SYNOPSIS

- Many Western parishes lack young people, have exhausted clergy and find mission too arduous.
- A parish's fundamental question must be: What do we do for our community?
- Doing things well in a community brings new growth.
- Many parishes ask the wrong question "what do we need? They should ask "What do we offer"?
- Different generations in a society have different needs and must be provided with different initiatives.
- Global and Diocesan events (World Youth Day/Diocesan events) are useful for mission, but only if they have serious local follow-up.
- Schools attached to parishes are not natural "feeders" for your parish. Additional connections of youth workers and parent support are also needed.
- Specific leadership teams must be developed for school connections and youth under 25 years of age. Local leadership is best for these groups, not paid employees.

8

ACHIEVING EARLY WINS

A parish that proposes new ventures, strategies and programs must ensure that they achieve some early victories and at least small measurable successes. In the inception stage of a new strategy these "runs on the board" have little to do with encouraging those involved with the new program, but everything to do with giving the uncommitted and wider parish members reassurance and confidence in your overall competence. Programs that fail do not normally do so because the immediate program participants lacked energy. In most cases, failure results from misunderstanding, cynicism or lack of support from the wider elements of a parish. Above all, changes must result in reassurance and a feeling that parish leaders are undertaking worthwhile plans in a reliable and committed way.

I have witnessed too many parishes with new management plans or styles that are quick to demolish or downplay all that has gone before, activate new and innovative programs only to see them fail because they failed to establish the key element on which all success is built: Reassurance.

Reassurance and confidence in measures cannot be achieved overnight. The immediate challenge in parishes is usually only about the need to change – you are still a long way from actual change. Actual change can only be assured through the development and growth in reassurance and confidence from the wider parish. Without such trust you will fail.

This trust can only be attained by parishioners seeing and agreeing that you have had some wins and that your early plans are working. Unfortunately the excitement of planning, developing and implementing new programs often means that the important first steps are rushed or involve grasping at changes beyond initial capability.

The main characteristic of rushed implementation often results from the temptation to implement a "grand plan" all in the first six weeks! Certainly it is important to have a clearly articulated grand plan, yet it is equally important not to stampede its implementation and guarantee its failure.

In any strategic plan, change is resisted. This is normal, it's not personal. It is the nature of the majority of human beings. We live by patterns and we get used to local "normality" which we like to be assured is unchanging. Most human beings will agree with the value and benefits to be gained from changes, it's just not something they actually wish to do often or something they think others should undertake first.

If you really wish for change to occur in your parish you must ensure that reassurance is a central plank. Change that fails to engender support or achieve its outcomes makes future success with other changes less likely. The first changes you make must be ones in which you can demonstrate some success, no matter how small!

It is also fundamental, that you stay within parameters that can be achieved by you. By this I mean, the work you undertake and the initiative you undertake will be seen by others as yours. That's an important first step, but only if you make them work! The wins must be yours and you must ensure you claim them. This is essential to your credibility and future success.

Consequently, there are a few things you should not do despite the temptation. Do not attempt to fix or repair long standing black holes. These are the events, personalities or problems that usually have been with a parish for a significant period. Others have crashed upon these rocks; you must ensure you do not add yourself to the list.

Resolving long standing issues or attempting to smooch locals who have resisted or rejected ideas in the past should not be an opening invitation. These can wait; your first and central task is to establish a winning culture around new ideas; a new priest or a new committee. Most individuals who have been problematic outsiders for a number of years, have learnt to enjoy the role, whatever the founding grievances, their response to new beginnings will usually be more opposition. If this has become their principal reason for being, initial opposition won't change. Your only hope, at a later date, is to appeal to them afresh, but to appeal from a position of strength and success. Establish a winning culture first.

In these early stages, it is important to hasten slowly, but to nevertheless be consistent. My preference with parish initiatives is to choose and commence something that has not been attempted locally before. This will require some thorough study and analysis, but picking a niche or a gap in the parish or community offering demonstrates to others that you are not on about change for change sake. New initiatives must have a strong impression around them that suggests growth, it you can find niche markets without competition; your emphasis on growth will be significantly stronger. If you seek to commence something that is already a significant success in another church or district you risk comparison to them, both as they are now and as they were at comparable stages. If you undertake to commence something already existing elsewhere, that's fine, as long as you can make substantial arguments as to why your program is really "different".

At the advent of your new program, words that indicate difference, progressiveness, wide-ranging, naturalness or world's-first are all your friends. They strongly convey the impression that you have re-invented the wheel. Many parishioners long to do something in parishes that is different, game-changing and makes a difference, these are the people whose support you need. There will be many parishioners content to remain on flower rosters, working bees and after mass cups of tea. In the first instance you must attract the enthusiasm of those really wanting to undertake change and make a difference.

Secondly, it is essential to flood your parish with propaganda, this is not a brainwashing exercise – in fact it is exactly the opposite. Constant information about the programs intentions, the personnel involved, the enthusiasm of the participants all seek to engender greater enthusiasm within the wider parish for what you are doing. Essentially, you are providing a sense of pride in your work to as many people, inside and outside your parish as possible.

This is not a bragging exercise; rather this consistent stream of information is an important motivation, for those involved in the day to day running and planning of your programs. If you do not constantly promote and re-promote your program you risk the high probability that program leaders will feel under-appreciated, won't be valued by others and may find excuses to not continue when initial enthusiasm wanes. The promotion, advertising and publicity for your programs is the responsibility of the priest and his pastoral council. Parishes who feel such an approach is conceited and egotistical are failing to understand how voluntary organisations work. Without substantial praise to those who work with you (in their own time) you ensure you won't have them for long. Unfortunately, this is the central reason that many well-intentional and worthwhile initiatives in parishes fail: not enough care and nurture was generated for those involved. At this point, it is not about making the priest feel good, but supporting the community members who actually do the work. Silence is not golden; it ensures failure. Ultimately, most parish programs fail because they start with great enthusiasm and energy only to find this vitality slump within a few months.

It is important to maintain *constant activity* across your program, this usually means little changes and adaptation each week or two, the addition of new staff or a slight refocus on the program's objective. Very few parishes do this well, these little disruptions must be managed and deliberately encouraged. They are the key ingredient that sustains motivation and a sense of achievement. Without constantly tweaking, changing the order or evolving the roles of staff, burnout and indifference will soon set in and programs collapse when "indispensable" leaders move on. Allowing a variety of different individual's leadership roles is an important aspect of maintaining your programs as fresh and innovative. Naturally, this costs time and effort in continually, developing, coaching and encouraging others to step into unfamiliar roles. Without this leadership rotation and evolution, the long-term stability of voluntary programs is at risk. The great problem confronting most parishes is finding energising leaders. This does not happen by accident, they don't walk in the door, you have to build and sustain them from within. In my view all parishes must consider locally run leadership courses as a matter of priority, yet most parishes don't do this. I have little sympathy when these same parishes talk of parish decline and decay. Your own back yard is the place where this is repaired.

ACHIEVING EARLY WINS: SYNOPSIS

- New programs must have small early and measurable success.
- Small early success generates parish confidence.
- Early failure usually results from misunderstandings, cynicism or lack of support. Energy is the most important attribute for success.
- Small success builds wider reassurance of greater future success.
- Change takes time, major initiatives without smaller early success guarantees failure.
- Parishes that do not "own small initiatives make future success unlikely.
- Attempting to resolve long standing issues first makes wider success unlikely: Establish a winning culture first.
- An emphasis on "niche" programs and identifying gaps demonstrates "targeted" change, emphasising you seek to make a difference without "change for changes sake"
- Constant updated information in relation to new programs encourages enthusiasm and support.
- Failure to support and encourage your new programs leads to people feeling unappreciated and burning out.

9

VOCATION AND MISSION

There is an increasing tendency in many parishes to present the primary work of the parish as one that endeavours to satisfy the needs of parishioners. Parishes that do this make a substantial error.

The proliferation of billboards erected on churches proclaiming the solution to human problems is usually an indication of a church which has chosen this path. Are you lonely? Are you depressed? Are you anxious? These are all aspects of a church that has chosen to represent itself to the world as one concerned with the individual, but with a focus that sees problem solving and self-improvement as its primary role. The Catholic Church has only ever seen this as part of the story. Although it is popular to see religion as all about getting your needs met, the Catholic view has never been that this is an essential part of our relationship with God. The Catholic view has always been a vocational one, what is God calling me to do? What is my vocation to be?

For Catholics our relationship to God has always been much deeper, what is God calling you to do? You have a vocation; it's your job to discover what it is. God does not just call you to come to mass, as central as that is, he also calls you to do and to be someone for him in a unique way.

The true freedom of the Catholic life is the discovery of vocation and that requires a different question from us. Jesus, what do you want from us?

We have a choice of what we make Jesus to be. Do we make him a kind of errand boy whose key role is to satisfy our needs or are we more Catholic in perspective seeing this relationship as one where we also have something to do.

The Catholic Church baptises and confirms many thousands of

individuals each year across every diocese, yet, a fundamental question remains: Where are they now? Why have we failed to maintain people on their journey of faith beyond the initial enthusiastic period. In my view, the failure to sustain the faith is related to the development and understanding of vocation. When individuals are unable to recognise, develop and sustain a vocation, they are at greater risk of unwittingly seeing their faith wither and potentially die.

The greatest question we can ask ourselves as Catholics is what is my vocation? What am I called to do? How can my vocation help my local parish community? Discover these answers and you will have a vital and useful expression of the faith.

As a result of the centrality of vocation to Christian life, it is vitally important that parishes take concrete actions to encourage the vocation of all of their parishioners. It is not priests alone who have a vocation, in fact, priestly vocation is but a slither of the manifold vocation that God gives to his people for sustaining and building a parish. An important part of priesthood and parish leadership is fostering the sense of vocation in your parishioners. If you only develop programs designed to satisfy needs or alleviate problems you are only doing half a job.

In this sense, the discovery, identification and encouraging of vocation needs organisation. The work of distilling vocation is usually neglected in modern parish life. This needs to change. An important beginning can be made with the creation of a designated "vocations" representative or the formation of a specific sub-committee to harness, direct and encourage local vocations centred on your parish. Many of your parishioners will have never considered the vocational aspect of the Christian life and some will even suggest that they have no vocation or specific calling from God. It will be necessary to talk regularly about the needs of the parish, but also about the nature of vocation and how central it is to both individual and parish life. Parishes are failing because we talk endlessly about the importance and duty involved in mass attendance, but we then do little to sustain people in their daily faith life. Generally, we do not leave our parishioners with the expertise to generate or perfect a vocational life, nor emphasise how important this is to the life of faith. All Catholics are called to a life of mission and building of the local Catholic community. By not talking or acting on this dimension we send two subconscious messages, firstly mission is not important and secondly, vocation and calling are something that only happen to priests.

The most obvious question to arise once such discussions commence in a parish is "What can I do?" or "What do you want me to do?" This is not an exercise in giving people jobs to perform around the parish. This is an exercise in mission. Certainly, general parish needs, programs and future plans should be laid out before parishioners, many of them will certainly feel called to participate and contribute to existing programs or suggestions from a leadership group.

Nevertheless, vocation is much more than this. It requires patience, has numerous false starts and travels along unforeseen paths. Primarily this is about developing and sustaining the individual's hopes and skills, allowing them to see God's specific call to them and then looking at ways to possibly channel this vocation into the wider life of the local parish. Vocation must always be acted upon. There are too many Catholics, talking, discussing and planning and then doing nothing! In this instance, the role of the vocational representative or leadership group is two-fold, to help individuals tease out the concept, meaning and practice of vocation and then most importantly offer individuals practical, local and meaningful ways to express this vocation. This may mean some individuals do things in other parishes which have existing activities that fit their vocation. The greatest gift of the Holy Spirit awaits not so much in funnelling "workers" into existing programs, but in allowing the Holy Spirit to prompt, suggest and stimulate new ways of engaging between your local parish, the surrounding community and the programs you may offer into the future.

Parishioners grow and develop through existing parishioners bringing along new people or families, yet more common is the opportunity to engage with your parish through something you do. It is in these mission activities that the concept of vocation is strongest, and the energy of the individual can be placed firmly at the disposal of the local parish. A vocational dimension to your parish requires clear thinking, hard consistent work and specific training.

The leadership group must be clear on the specific goals and plans of the parish and importantly have the ability to articulate this clearly. Every program your parish undertakes must have a mission dimension. There is no benefit in undertaking programs where only existing parishioners will benefit. As brutal as it may seem, it is not enough to have a small youth group made up of a few children from families that already attend. This is no more than a starting point, the central question will always remain: "What have you built from the foundations you were given?" Therefore, it is important to know the goals and the direction of your programs.

Additionally, programs and parish groups should be task orientated and as practical as possible. Talk-fests, discussion groups or bible studies are not mission, if they only involve the already committed insiders. It is certainly appropriate to undertake studies that strengthen those already committed, but let's not pretend that this makes you busy with mission. Mission is about "doing" the things that bring people to you or that take you to others, it must be focused on the outsiders and it should also give wide scope to allow those of your own parish to be putting their vocation into place.

For this renewal of parish life to take place, both priests and leadership teams must have a regular focus on discovering and encouraging vocation. Priests in particular must teach and preach about the nature of God's calling to us. Always surprising and through the most unusual people. This takes skill and commitment, but cannot be neglected if significant or sustained renewal is to take place.

Finally, specific training must be made available to those whose "vocation" is to find and encourage the gifts of others. This training will always be different depending on the individuals involved, but it should have a few common characteristics. A strong desire to listen, an ability to take an initial idea and develop it within a practical dimension, the ability to encourage others and to connect those exploring a vocation into strong connections with those able to sustain and nurture ideas.

The fundamental concept of mission must always be one of service. Individual praise and admiration are important to encourage those seeking to understand their particular call to service, but they are not final goals. Very few modern parishes place any sustained emphasis on vocation and mission. Parishes without these concepts are mostly those exhibiting signs of collapse. They rely on the energy of individual priests or a small handful of committed parishioners. Vocation and mission are directed to all of us, anything less downplays Christ's vision for his Church "Go and make disciples of all Nations" (Matthew 24).

VOCATION AND MISSION: SYNOPSIS

- Satisfying the needs of parishioners is not mission.
- Catholicism is not primarily concerned with the needs of the individual but with developing vocation.
- The true freedom of Catholic life is the discovery of vocation and requires the question: "Jesus, What do you want from me?"
- The failure of individuals to sustain their faith is a failure of vocation.
- The greatest question we can ask ourselves as Catholics is "What is my vocation"?
- Parishes must take concrete steps to develop vocations in all parishes.
- Discovering, identifying and encouraging vocations needs organisation.
- Parishes should consider "vocation representatives" to develop and strengthen vocation.
- Individual vocations and connected parish programs should be as practical as possible – service is central.
- Parishes without vocation and mission will ultimately collapse.

10

THE PAST IS NOT A PARADISE

There is a common perception in some parishes that things were better or easier in other eras of the Churches life. This is dialogue that centres on days when the Church was full, when young people attended, when baptisms and confirmations took place in the thousands, priests were abundant and a real sense of community was evident. Parishes that regularly lament in this way are dead men walking.

In any parish community it is imperative that such laments are quickly challenged and banished from community conversations. Firstly, these regretful conversations are a requiem for your current and future life. They are in essence untrue and they subvert the teaching of Christ that he is with each generation to the end of time. More significantly, it suggests a serious disconnection with the culture in which your Church is imbedded or an intellectual opposition to the modern world.

The romantic period arose in the 18th and 19th centuries as an oppositional intellectual movement to the industrial revolution. It was distrustful of the human world, the speed of modern development and longed for a close connection with nature, which it viewed as morally less corrupting than human systems and intellectual life.

There are still a significant number of Catholics who long for this idealised past often as a reaction to the speed of life or the myriad sets of problems confronting most nations and the Church. But is this actually based on any truth? Such a negative view of our world of terrorism or drugs requires the overlooking of the destruction of the Nazis, the horror and persecution of millions by Communism, the economic depression of the 20's, the vastly reduced life spans, the hundreds of thousands of women who died in childbirth, the plagues of polio, TB and influenza. By any indicator of human wellbeing the modern world is undoubtedly the best time to be alive.

In a similar manner parishes need to capture a sense that today's opportunities for mission, for parish growth, for religious communities to make profound contributions to societal life, are greater today than at any time in our history.

This is not to suggest an emphasis on the modern word is inimical to Catholic traditions. Our traditions are our unique beliefs, celebrations, religious holidays and symbolic ways of understanding the world. Yet, more importantly Catholic traditions and sacramental life are the means given to us to participate in the life of the trinity itself, to engage with Christ and his teachings and to reform our community life anew. The nature of these traditions is unchanging, yet they must always be made relevant for each generation. Parishes that use liturgical language based on theological concepts from Tudor English times signal strongly that they are not interested in engaging the modern world or its young people. This is a form of vandalism to Christ's teaching. They deserve the extinction they face. If you will not engage with the current world, speak its language and use its modern methods of communication then a serious question arises, for whom does your parish exist? It is hard to see such a parish existing to make disciples of all nations.

The secular world uses a series of stereotypes against the Church. These are commonly based on sentiment which suggests the Church is not modern or relevant, lives only in the past, concentrates on tradition to the exclusion of participating in real-world solutions and seeks only to control people by using dogma as a weapon against change. We do need to acknowledge that these sentiments are present in our mostly secular societies. We also need to recognise that they can be confronted and that they must be, if we are to engage with those in our wider world.

Within the context of secular Australia, the community has witnessed a number of national celebrations which within our recent past have seemed to be almost eradicated from public life, but have over the last 25 years made unpredictable and significant recovery. Anzac Day is the most striking example of this revival. The national day of remembrance for Australians and New Zealanders who served and died in all wars was in serious trouble in the 1970's, and post the Vietnam War, indifference to Anzac commemorations saw poor attendance at Anzac marches and services.

This has changed dramatically in the last 25 years, the commemorations have become strongly identified with both our national character and our purpose and place in the wider world. Australians see themselves as tough, resilient and prepared to undertake difficult military operations in the defence of their freedom, liberty and the future of others suffering oppression. These values are almost exclusively taken from Anzac traditions and example.

How has this transformation happened? Importantly, public interaction was significantly increased. The influence of connections with sport should not be downplayed; particularly the advent of the annual Essendon and Collingwood Australian football match, now adopted by many other football codes and community events. The relevance and substance of Anzac day was given renewed significance through its connection with activities loved by many Australians. Anzac Day was transformed and returned to a central social status through its connection with an apparently ordinary activity: sport. The Church should take note, there is no sense complaining that our importance in national life, or our historical centrality to society is downplayed, if we are no longer connected to the daily ordinary events of everyday people. This is the fundamental problem confronting the Catholic Church; we are no longer connected to the ideals, hopes and concerns of ordinary people. In consequence, we have no influence within the lives of most Australians. Rather than moving to an elite or club like appearance, we must return to the ordinary concerns and passions upheld by most Australians. Then we may have something significant to offer!

Perhaps the transformation of Anzac Day was not the result of a coordinated or calculated plan. Nevertheless, since noting the goodwill of the Australian population towards the renewed purpose of Anzac celebrations, intentional, deliberate and purposed events have developed throughout the nation and overseas. Battlefield tours, war memorial celebrations in France, connection with school communities in places where Australians fought, fundraising for memorials and community halls, the building of new schools, exchanges of students, teachers, choirs have all resulted in stronger connections between communities who once shared significant adversity. None of this has resulted in a trivialization of the nature of the Anzac tradition.

There are important implications for the Church in the transformation of the Anzac tradition. Primarily it asks the question, can we as parish communities hold events within our churches that celebrate local events and or highlight local concerns? The Church has traditionally transformed secular events and celebrations (Christmas an obvious example) into something of more lasting purpose and meaning. Why have we stopped this transformational principle and approach to the secular world? After all, this is our fundamental vocation to transform society and undertake our mission imperative.

There should be a number of key intentional areas of focus, we must be concerned with youth and families as a priority. This challenges us to present our tradition in ways that can be understood and made relevant to younger generations. Younger people are extremely pro-active in their uptake of modern technology and ideas, if our traditions do not have this packaging we cannot expect to speak to this generation in any meaningful way. Parishes might consider that we lock away almost all of our religious observances in church buildings that can only be viewed by "insiders". Why not consider increasing outdoor celebrations, in public view that allow the uncommitted or those who have never heard of Catholics, an entry participation without compromising our beliefs or presenting ourselves as only looking for new converts.

Recently, whilst visiting Thailand, I experienced the lantern festival of Loi Krathong on full moon. As Christians who celebrate the coming of the Holy Spirit, we do not have an obvious public celebration for such an event. It is not possible for local parishes on parks or beaches to offer non-Christians the chance to participate in a "Christianised" flying lantern service which celebrates the gift of the Holy Spirit.

The possibilities of adaptation are endless, but there must be opportunities for parishes to interact with non-parishioners in ways that reveals something of our beliefs without compromise to our major celebrations. Above all, they must have a modern outlook; this will undoubtedly mean an approach that concentrates on social media, twitter communication and other modern "word of mouth" avenues. These are prime opportunities for young parishioners to drive new events and "teach" others within our communities new methods of connecting with and transforming our society. The only substantial change that needs to take place in any "standard" parish is the desire to take risks in connecting to the wider community.

THE PAST IS NOT A PARADISE: SYNOPSIS

- Laments that the past was better destroy the present and future.
- Today's opportunities for mission and parish growth are greater than at any time in our history.
- Our traditions are central but must remain relevant for each generation.
- Secular agencies often paint the Church as irrelevant, old fashioned and dogmatic. Parishes must challenge this thinking.
- Secular celebrations such as Anzac Day have changed over the years by re-connecting with community, sports and everyday life.
- Parishes might consider a greater number of religious observances in the "public domain.
- Social media plays a major role in hosting and developing outside events that can be "shared" by non-Christians.

11

MEMBERSHIP AND PARTICIPATION

On any given vigil or Sunday mass it is not difficult to assess your weekly mass attendance. How many people do you have attending at your 10am mass? Is it more than last week? Last year? or five years ago? This analysis gives some guide to the health of your parish, yet in my view this is a notoriously unreliable snapshot of the participation and commitment to your parish. For many reasons generalised attendance figures can vary substantially, a visiting bishop, a holiday season, a school commencement service or graduation, a special guest speaker, an important festival. All of these factors can potentially enlarge or distract from your numbers at mass. In my view generalising mass numbers are an unhelpful indicator for gauging commitment or participation in your parish.

Of much more importance is figures on the financial commitment of the individuals that attend your masses. These benefactors are the real backers, supporters and patrons of your parish. Let's not be too crude but anyone can say they support Essendon Football Club and reap some benefits and enjoyment when the team wins, but these are not your true supporters. True supporters are the ones that are prepared to put something of themselves into your club; their money. It is the same for a parish, financial commitment is the strongest indicator of long-term commitment and support for the faith, ideals and future of the parish. After all, you don't put your money into something that won't be around in five years' time. Those who commit their money see a future, for you, for themselves and their children.

Whilst most parishes don't have official members in reality, those involved in your stewardship programs and those who commit their financial resources are your members. It is no longer good enough to run stewardship and finance programs without addressing the fundamental question: What are you expecting your people to give to? What are your aims and objectives for your Parish? And most importantly are you indicating to your potential donors that you are expecting to be around for another 100 years. Unfortunately, what passes for most parish finance programs is little more than a maintenance schedule. These upkeep programs amount to little more than paying the bills, maintaining the priest and fixing minor issues with buildings either within the presbytery or on the church building and plant.

Nevertheless, the choice of running such a program has huge psychological impacts on your community. If we think clearly, what are we actually saying about our parish future. We have no great plans or expectations for the future, we are seeking to hold on to what we have and our place within our community. We expect no growth and we are focused on those members who currently attend our services. As we do not subconsciously expect any growth to occur, it is safe to conclude that parishes' resources and needs will stay around the same percentage as last year. This begs the obvious question, why join a parish which doesn't see itself as going anywhere into the future?

If you run a program within your parish that asks for financial commitment, do not focus on upkeep, utility, bills, the rising costs of maintenance or the stipend for the priest. If you do this you are subconsciously indicating you have no future.

A critical question now arises, what alternatives will your leadership team offer as incentives for fundraising which do not underline maintenance and general upkeep?

Of primary importance should be an emphasis on values. These principles must be ethical but, most significantly, programs must highlight the ability of your parish to make a difference to society, to young people and to transform your parish.

These values must be future driven, they should emphasise the long-term nature of your parish and demonstrate how you will transform your community, bringing people out of difficulty or change people's lives. These are the underlying motives which drive and inspire an influential parish. Give your parishioners a parish that makes a difference, changes lives and promotes a culture of action, all within a better and brighter future.

There are a number of important assumptions behind this emphasis on values. Firstly changing the community is not just for yourself, it's primarily for future generations. These are essential propositions if you wish your parish to be seen as permanent, stable and a vital pillar of your society 100 years from now.

Be positive: people want to give to positive organisations that are long-lasting and that change lives. It is important to highlight an important change that has taken place in your parish and how others see you. The question directed towards your parish from your parishioners must never be "what can they do for me"? But "what can I do for them" as they seek to change the community, society and a parish life together.

This emphasis on positive and future orientated values requires a profound change in the attitudes of many parish communities.

It is easy to see what's wrong with the world, it is easy to see your own difficulties, but these must be set aside if strong faith and trust connections are really waiting to be built.

Unfortunately, most parishes erode this emotional and faith connection by highlighting fear as a primary gauge of community life. We need to stick together as we are a remnant society. While the world goes crazy we will stick to our values, we are calling on you to help us financially and if we cannot successfully raise this money we will be forced to close our doors! We are a community that has been here for 100 years; don't let us be the last. The assumption behind all these subconscious views, is that we are a people of the past, we are no longer connected to our community and we have no significant long-term future.

Negativity in parish life can be hard to defeat unless you are constantly able to clearly identify and uphold your basic parish membership goals. It is especially important that these values are supported in the face of local opposition that may arise from time to time. Primarily, you must keep emphasising your key goals.

Secondly: You must have a commitment to youth. Lots of parishes say this but in reality they only mean that things will stay the same, but young people will magically attend and sit quietly! A strong emphasis on youth requires a radically different psychology and a desire to make changes that allow young people into position of authority with the ability to make changes and innovate. The "connectedness" of young people is radically different from any previous generation and the possibilities for peer to peer connection far outweigh anything imagined by the average priest or parish. If we are able to allow innovative thinking and a path for creative ideas to emerge, we will see the centrality of Christ presented in new and significant ways. The truth within parish life is that few young people are trusted, valued or encouraged to make a difference. It is not surprising they have found the parish environment boring, not related to their interests and wandered away. Parishes that are unable or unwilling to include under 20's centrally in their structures, and support their ideas are not sufficiently thinking of the future. Within the Australian context, we have now lost two generations, those 45 years old to 60 years and their children usually 16-25 years of age. When will we act to engage with what is now the vast majority of Australians. We need an attitude change that encourages younger Australians and commits us to their future.

Thirdly: Membership and participation is about friendship. The notion of parishioners as friends and community is much talked about, but rarely a reality. What is a reality is the high number of individuals who attend mass but then can't wait to leave. Many masses, sermons and the music presented for them are boring, disorganised and intellectually sentimental. The situation in most parishes is that those who attend don't know each other and often don't have the time investment needed to engage with their parish community. In many Catholic parishes the concept of "community" is extremely weak and the parish is a passionless place filled with people going through the motions. If that was not the case, our numbers for mass attendance would be higher.

Consequently, the attitude of parish leadership must be prepared to change. We cannot always ask for money, in fact, we must communicate our ideas, values and future plans twice as much as we ask for money. If we don't have an underlying attitude that we are here to "learn from you", then what sort of partnership are we talking about within our parish! Mass is the most important sacrament within Catholic life, but we constantly must encourage those who come to not only see sacramental life as an individual responsibility, but as also as joining with friends on the journey and fighting for a common cause. If we cannot convey the unique, local nature of parish life, then it will be impossible to financially move beyond "maintenance money". I will give maintenance money to keep the show going, so that I can continue to get what I want – a weekly mass. The much more significant question is "What does this community do? What are the values of the parish as a collective? It is only a community vision that allows individual responses to it. Jesus created communities designed to go into the future and engage with it. Only a community vision of that future can bring about this reality for a local parish. If we are not friends together and partners to our parish community then we will not have a meaningful future that can engage with others.

Fourthly: Most funding and membership models focus on building a base of consistent supporters, yet much more important is getting the "right" people. The "right" people are those who buy into the wider parish vision and are able to picture a future. They are people energized to think in different ways and apply fresh solutions to local problems as they arise. These are individuals with strong relationships to others and a willingness to establish and encourage new relationships and to bring outsiders in. Nevertheless, they must have a message to promote.

Too many parishes seem concerned only with acquiring a small commitment from as wide a range as possible. Yet, the truth of our parish life is that usually we are missing the "energizers" that enable the passion on which futures are built. It is easy to suggest that parishes filled mostly with retirees and people on fixed incomes are unable to lift financial contributions significantly. This is partly true, nevertheless it is also accurate to suggest that most leadership teams are not looking to encouraging energizers or to demonstrate that such a role within a parish community is a vocation. If we do not highlight, celebrate and esteem such roles within parish life, then we will never find them. A major concern in many parishes is our constant success at burying our talents. This applies to our people as well. If we attract, energise and enthuse our people with a purposeful vision, financial support and fundraising are no longer a troublesome difficulty, but are part of the passion for driving success.

Finally: Membership and participation are also strongly related to a substantial media profile. Local parishioners are capable of undertaking and sustaining such a commitment, especially through local media outlets who are usually desperate for human interest, festival and other event information. To do this in a determined fashion does require designated parishioners to be charged with this leadership and responsibility. The parish must make a commitment to having a continuous stream of news, events and proposals ready for distribution to the surrounding local community and neighbourhood agencies. Additionally, membership brochures, bequest brochures and direct mail should not be overlooked. This media and communication approach should be all about raising the profile of your parish and commitment to the people of your region. Each request for money should portray a positive message and a hopeful and opportunistic future. In this sense, no communication with parishioners, associates or the wider community is wasted. Even if no money is raised in this fashion, profile will be.

Importantly, parish communication and use of media must proudly exhibit your core values, specific actions, your viability and your importance for the future of your region and its future.

MEMBERSHIP AND PARTICIPATION: SYNOPSIS

- Mass attendance is a poor indicator of parish health – the numbers who commit financially are a greater indicator of "true supporters".
- Financial support is closely related to clear, concise and understandable parish goals and objectives.
- Operating community programs tells parishioners and

outsiders that you intend to be around for the "long journey".
- Parishes without community programs subconsciously indicate they are concerned only with themselves and have no long-term community plans.
- Financial giving programs should not be based on models of maintenance or paying bills, but focus strongly on future driven youth programs.
- Parish programs should emphasise values, ethics and making a difference to society.
- Parish programs should highlight the long lasting nature of your parish and your work for families, children and future generations.
- Parish culture must encourage thinking away from "what can this parish do for me"? to "how can I help the parish change our community"?
- Parish culture which talks about surviving as "remnant" community erodes its future, attracts negativity and fails to connect with younger people.
- Trust young people in leadership roles and support innovative ideas, be prepared to learn from them.
- Parishioners who give consistently are important, yet greater importance is located in energising the "right people", that is, those who are future driven, can apply fresh solutions to local problems and who establish strong relationships.
- Parishioners of energy and passion are central. Encourage and support them.
- Parishes must have a commitment to media relationships. These support your programs, attract new people and sustain the energy of your parishioners.

12
PARISH LEADERSHIP

"No Institution can possibly survive if it needs geniuses or supermen to manage it. It must be organised in such a way as to be able to grow and thrive under a leadership of average human beings" -- Peter Drucker

Leadership is perhaps the most overstated requirement in the life of the Church. If we are honest within the historical framework and into our present time, leadership at parish or diocesan level often sees the focus on finding an outstanding leader as little more than an exercise in passing the buck.

Plainly, within particular parishes there have been priests and parish lay leaders who have managed to provide vision, purpose and energy to enthuse people and to build structures that have endured across generations, but this is not the norm.

The most common experience in parish leadership is one of preservation, upkeep and continuation of things started and developed by past leadership initiatives. In a fast changing world with many parishes in which large numbers of people migrate or relocate through a parish in only a few years, constant amendment and refreshment must be a central focus. It is here that most parish leadership is tested and often stalls. They key dimension of parish leadership must be a focus on adapting to change, but even more importantly stimulating the movement of change so that local adaptations are trend setting and not constantly reactive.

Nevertheless, before considering such issues there are a number of ways that parish and church leadership are different from other forms of organisational leadership. Of critical importance for parish leadership is to be seen, be available and be present. Any parish priest or lay leader that is not able or prepared to be "within" the lives of their parishioners is ineffectual and undone before ministry can actually start.

The reality for parish leadership is that success comes from sharing the load and experience of your people. Priests and lay leaders must be available within 12-24 hours of events happening. Any crisis that is undergone within individuals or the wider parish must be shared by the leadership group. In my work with chaplaincy being quickly seen or available lends credibility to your role that cannot be gained or developed one or two weeks later. The message is simple, if someone in your parish is involved in a car crash, get to the site, hospital or home immediately. This enables people to feel you went through an experience with them. Even if little effective comfort or counselling can be offered, they will remember later that you were there. Turning up two days later for the first time and expecting to be valuable or relevant is highly unconvincing – Creditability in parish leadership is acquired from being present and involved at the outset. This is the central element of successful parish leadership and ministry. Without this dimension, you may be an organised, well run, financially stable parish, but you will not gain loyalty or passion from your people and it will be difficult to affect long-term meaningful change.

Unfortunately, this dimension can be downplayed by some parish leaders, who imagine that leadership is primarily to be found in robust systems, or in a business style aloofness, that lives beyond the fray. The parish business is a trust business; if you can't or won't get your hands dirty, then others will have little expectation that they should do so on your behalf. A priest or leadership team that stops visiting and only "sees" those that attend on Sunday faces extinction.

Unfortunately as many corporate leaders have only discovered to their peril you need engagement with your people. A parish leadership team that doesn't do this basic activity will not be able to complete meaningful or life-changing work. It is my strong contention that parish leadership can be effective, life changing and doesn't require hugely skilled, educated or talented individuals; it does require people who are prepared to be persistent, resilient and not put off easily. These are the key traits of successful leadership teams; yet, the greatest crime in parish leadership is not attempting to make a difference. Too many parishes do nothing, never change and each year looks like the last one. The Gospel imperative is to preach to all people. This means being in your community, being alongside your people. Those parishes that are clubs for insiders are indeed rewarded, perhaps in maintaining their bank accounts or lovely buildings, but they will be missing the essential ingredient: people who love Jesus and who wish to make a difference!

In my experience, many parishes contain an undercurrent of fear. This may be fear of failure, fear of not living up to past achievements or fear of being the last group of parishioners at a particular church. Many parishes have this underlying residue of fear. Recently, a new layer of hesitancy has entered some parish communities, particularly those who have experienced dimensions of clergy abuse. There are certainly many reasons not to undertake life changing programs or new ideas – and yes, there will always be plenty of people quick to criticise or mock your early efforts and highlight your failures.

A key way of overcoming fear is to remove it from the "thinking" stage. Too many parish leadership groups over think the problems and likely resisters and also worry about how things "look" to others.

Naturally, this kind of thinking often results in little movement or activity: so here is a new motto for parishes in such a situation. *Don't think! Do!*

Strong and successful leadership teams are aware of failure, they've just forgotten when it happened because they have sufficient success to persist, and success, of course brings more energy, a renewed ability to keep trying and a greater willingness to engage with those outside their parish.

All successful parishes have one thing in common- they make the decision to act, not wait, look or hope for better timing. Almost all of these early actions were clumsy and probably only involved partial success, but it was enough success to want more. This is another important ingredient in understanding leadership- a little bit of success will give you the courage to want more, encourage you to spend time making things better and help to unite your parish around greater unity and a vision of the future.

Successful parish leadership makes the assumption that you will make mistakes and lots of them. All successful human beings and corporations have myriad layers of failure. The importance of failure is to make sure it becomes a driver for future success not a blockage to trying nothing in the future. One of my favourite politicians is Winston Churchill, who some would consider to be the most significant individual of the twentieth century. There is much to be gained from a quick précis of his life, a life ironically that was overwhelmingly full of failure. At twenty years of age Churchill was a hopeless academic failure who had not gained his higher School Certificate. An officer cadet only at his third attempt, an embarrassment to his family and in his dying father's opinion a total "washout". Yet, by 25 years of age he had become a war hero, written two acclaimed books and taken his first steps on a lifelong political career.

What changed in this short period of time? In his own words he realised that he must now become "master of my own fortune".

Churchill had correctly realised that he must be in charge of his own future, his own vocation, the need to discover and execute the future would be totally in his hands. No amount of wealth, education, or family connections could give him any of the things that are really important, ye he also realised that the only power source for such a journey could come from himself.

Whilst his somewhat self-centered sense of drive and ambition was not driven by a connection with Christ, the basic fundamentals for success are similar for any parish community:

- No-one will ever help you if you are unwilling to help yourself.
- Successful parish life is attained only through a willingness to try things.
- Financial security will only come after you have something "to do".
- Others will join you when they see consistent attempts "to do".
- Internal motivation can only come from your own leadership group.

The opposite of these initiatives is also true - new people will not join your parish unless they can see both your passion and actions towards future growth and will only give you financial support when they can see your commitment and persistence to your vision. Anything else is just a maintenance model that will only ever be partially supported.

Within a parish life, the greatest crime will always remain not attempting change.

A fruitful future does not occur when the timing is right. It needs to be taken and grasped.

Leadership within a parish context must generally be driven by the people who are already available, shining knights riding into your parish are a very rare phenomenon. The motivation to develop and advance your parish can only come from within, but it is important to encourage individuals with passion, resilience and strong desire to try and try again to step forward for this work. The choice Christ himself makes in the twelve disciples suggests talent and skills are not central prerequisites – only faithfulness and hard work matter.

The Catholic model of leadership suggests leaders are made not born. The challenge for all Christian leadership is to find and encourage individuals of hard work and passion. Parishes that foster this model find there is no such thing as a low talent pool.

PARISH LEADERSHIP: SYNOPSIS

- The leadership of many parishes is often well meaning but ineffectual.
- Poor leadership is concerned primarily with the preservation of past initiatives.
- Visualising and preparing for change is a healthier outcome than reacting to it.
- Priests and leadership teams that are unseen within the parish and wider community will be unsuccessful.
- Leadership success comes from "sharing the load" and trusting your people.

- Leadership credibility is only gained from being present and involved at the outset.
- "Getting your hands dirty" is more valuable leadership than establishing and operating systems.
- Persistence and resilience are more important than talent and skills in leadership teams.
- The greatest crime in leadership is not failure, but not attempting.
- Over-thinking leadership groups cause inertia. Don't think: Do!
- Successful parishes make decisions to act, not look, wait or hope for better timing.
- A little bit of success leads to greater accomplishments.
- Successful leadership teams operate on the assumption they will make mistakes.
- Failure is an important driver of future success.
- No-one will help you if you are unwilling to help yourself.
- Successful parish life is attained only through a willingness to try things.
- Financial security comes only after you "do" something.
- Others will join you when they see consistent attempts to "do".
- Long lasting motivation comes from within.
- An effective model of Leadership suggests leaders are made not born – there is no such thing as a low talent pool.

13
THE INVISIBLE PARISH

The regrettable truth for many parishes in the western world is that they are unknown and inconsequential to the majority of residents in their neighbourhoods.

This invisibility rises sharply when individuals under 35 years of age are considered. Unquestionably, the experience of most Australian young people not educated in Catholic Schools will be a minimal experience with the inside of a church, no knowledge of basic Catholic teachings, and a concept of the Church informed more by Harry Potter movies than any meaningful experience.

Additionally, the media landscape, in all predominately secular Western countries has turned aggressively anti-Catholic. This ensures that the editorial bias of mainstream media outlets, attaches negative connotations to stories surrounding the Church. This happens even to stories considered by church members to be favourable towards Catholic life and praxis.

It is a common experience of bishops, diocesan agencies and church spokespeople that there is a difficulty in connecting directly with uncommitted fellow Australians without an anti-Catholic filter on many news stories. Church attempts to put out media releases and positive articles are generally ignored.

It is in consequence, an urgent and pressing task that the Church finds alternative ways of connecting directly with those outside the Church, former adherents, inquiring individuals and a way of correcting misinformation and hostility.

The remorselessly negative press surround the substantial number of clergy abuse cases has meant that Catholics have become hesitant in advocating things they believe in across wider society. This has ensured that further Catholic contributions to community debate are not put into the public space or not pursued with sufficient vigour.

The public environment in some regions sees anti-discrimination legislation being used to prevent Catholics publically express their views. This has occurred most notably in Tasmania where trans-gender advocates lodged complaints against church booklets advocating for traditional marriage.

These new circumstances strongly suggest that direct appeal to those who seek relationship or connection with the Church is of vital importance. Social media is a significant opportunity to speak directly to adherents, the inquisitive, or general supporters without the overlay of media bias. In addition, this direct approach establishes a relationship with a wider community encourages a two-way conversation and further gives the Church opportunities to understand directly what people think. It also offers important possibilities to clarify a message or presentation in understandable ways.

Social media platforms such as Facebook and Instagram offer individual supporters the chance to share Catholic views with others, to build connections for your parish from individuals who were not previously familiar with your parish and to share mutually enriching articles, blogs or video clips. All of this strengthens the reach and influence of a Catholic parish.

For younger Australians, particularly under 35 years of age, this is a leading method of social contact, source of news, developing new interests and exposure to the opinions of others. Parishes that do not undertake to engage younger Australians in this way, not only indicate their indifference to this group, they remain invisible and subsequently meaningless to their way of thinking and behaviour. It is of paramount importance that the appearance and concepts exhibited on social media platforms are interesting and attractive to Australians under 35. You will achieve nothing with this group if you present outdated music, liturgy, sermons or irrelevant issues. A fundamental mistake constantly repeated in parishes is to imagine that younger Australians will automatically see the value of your parish if you present what you currently offer for over 55's. No-one will grow into this, they will only disengage. Churches that attempt to engage younger Australians through ancient English liturgy or music are treating mission as worthless and do damage to the future of their parish.

Subsequently, it is a necessity that you are well prepared with an offering relevant to the needs and interests of younger Australians. Don't go on social media to showcase what you already do. You must have new and captivating concepts, talks, music, speakers and deal with issues that are relevant and focused on under 35's. Invariably, this will mean substantial research and thought on those areas or needs you wish to target. The purpose of social media is not to fill your church with younger people, but to add a layer or network of interested people that have commenced a relationship with you. It may take years before substantial numbers of people do actually attend your parish. The primary purpose of social media is to create opportunities for contacts, develop trust, gentle teaching and encourage positive experiences. This process is not the end of mission, but its essential beginning. In no other format can such considerable numbers of mission opportunities be undertaken by comparatively small parish communities.

There are a number of obvious prerequisites that should be observed to secure successful entry into the world of social medial. Firstly, make sure your image to young people is energetic, vibrant and fresh. Pictures of older parishioners sharing cups of tea will guarantee a lack of success, yet this is the presenting image that so many parishes offer to the world. It is also an important message for outsiders to your parish to see photos of lots of activities outside your church building. To connect with the non-committed you must spend some time on their turf; parks, pubs, restaurants and schools, the hardest decision the non-committed will make is to enter through your parish door, the easier you make this action the easier future connections will be. Depictions of successful events with photos of people enjoyably engaging with each other are the necessary first steps to increasing connection with your parish.

Secondly, you should keep your "messaging" to one or two significant points. These do not necessarily need to be religious, but might concentrate on generalised concepts such as family or community. Such concepts are in short supply in many western countries and will resonate with many outsiders. Nevertheless, the most important outcome is not to overload social media presentations with lots of busy events that may overwhelm newcomers ,but keep the events of your parish specific and targeted.

Thirdly, you may as a thoughtful and reasoning parish consider a number of events that will be specifically linked to your social media presentation. Again, such events should be targeted to younger people and might include a number of events financially discounted to be attractive to those usually without substantial resources. Whilst it is reasonable to run social events, a much more attractive and powerful idea is to target the specific needs of your community. This may include mentoring, supporting, fundraising for charitable issues, or developing events to encourage change in areas of community distress. Younger Australians are particularly motivated to make a difference to adversity or local poverty. Astute parishes are able to identify such opportunities and provide intelligent and uncommon programs or events worthy of support.

Social media is a valuable tool of connection to a wider community beyond your parishioners, their families and extended families. It is another opportunity for your people to offer something to their community and to connect with others who support your basic values. Social media is also a benefit to your parish as greater understanding of your wider community and always leads to firmer and more powerful mission opportunities

THE INVISIBLE PARISH: SYNOPSIS

- The regrettable truth is that most parishes are not well known in their communities.
- This invisibility rises sharply in individuals under 35 years of age.
- Many secular media outlets are aggressively anti-Catholic.
- Catholics must find alternative ways to connect to their communities.

- Social media platforms offer an opportunity to speak directly to potential followers. For under 35's this is a leading source of news, opinion and social contact.
- Begin slowly: Social media should not attempt to fill your congregation with under 35's, but to add a layer of networked younger people: this is a beginning process in mission.
- Social media images must be young, energetic, vibrant and fresh.
- Concentrate on one or two significant and clear messages – don't be overly religious in the first instance.
- Link some specific events to your social media presentations – discount these events for younger people.
- Try to focus social media on "making a difference" – younger people are particularly motivated to make a difference in areas of adversity and local poverty.

14

IDENTIFY AND ENERGISE YOUR LEADERS

There is a great deal of talk throughout society on the need for leadership in political and economic life. The necessity to instruct, develop and encourage future leaders is also vital to the outlook and destiny of the Church.

The reality in many parishes is significantly underwhelming, leaders are hard to find, few are prepared to put their hands up for such roles and those that are engaged are often crushed into exhaustion.

Yet, no parish can grow, develop liturgy, or offer faith-filled programs that will make an affective impact on their local community, without a strong and united leadership group with sufficient numbers to secure a parish future.

The first specific truth to acknowledge is that there's no such thing as a parish that is "gifted" with leadership. God provides sufficient needs for every parish. The real question is: can local parishes identify and nurture the people within their midst or their extended network?

Many parishes complain that they are not able to attract children, families or youth, but before these essential groups can exist, there must be a serious desire for such outcomes. In my view, the essential parish contribution comes from aspiration: finance, buildings and leadership are all secondary. First, a parish must want and articulate a particular outcome. Leadership will follow and so the formula should be – aspirations – leadership - resources.

Many parishes make the mistake of saying, "we lack leadership, and therefore we cannot do". This attitude will ensure nothing ever happens. Firstly, the question should be "what is our need" or "what do we want to achieve?" Then the leadership to fulfil such ideas can be identified.

In recent years, a keenness to employ staff has arisen in many parishes. There is nothing wrong with this per se. However, this should not be an excuse for parishioners to hand over to pastoral assistant's duties and responsibilities that rightfully belong to them. Pastoral assistants should always be viewed as a specialist add-on, not as the core worker across a multitude of fields. At base, the majority of leadership roles should be filled with parishioners or seconded locals who are on-side with the parish goals and who are moving towards closer engagement with the parish. A warning note must be sounded in any parish where a handful of people are responsible for, or have acquired all leadership roles. This situation only leads to stagnation, inertia and lack of growth (100% of the time!!).

Leadership roles are required within an ever increasing number of parish tasks. Within a modern parish it is imperative to consider leadership in some key areas:

- Community
- Youth
- Planning (parish council)
- Administration
- Music
- Children
- Community Connectedness
- Motivation (encourage the doers)
- Elderly

This list can easily be added to, but it should not be less in an ideal world. Naturally, not all parishes are able to immediately consider or fulfil all of these undertakings with vibrant and skilled leadership and participants. Nevertheless, all parishes should have as a central goal, the desire to commence and operate such activities in the near future. Lack of desire or lack of persistence and intention is more problematic. Effectively this means your parish is not thinking or acting as a parish, instead you have become a club with all of the risks that entails for people who lack community connectedness.

As a matter of course, the type of leadership you wish for your parish is a significant question. This can also be a challenging question, particularly given that many parishes have previously used a model of leadership dependent only on the priest. Priests are responsible for the oversight and direction of their parishes, yet in modern societies, the skills, talents and leadership of parishioners cannot be overlooked. Successful parishes require a spread of effective leadership. Controlling or authoritarian priests will increasingly struggle to engage or inspire their parishioners to devote large swathes of their personal time to parish initiatives. The parish of the twenty-first century requires more sophistication, intricacy and equality in its leadership.

Overwhelmingly, priests and leadership teams should engage in prescriptive leadership-an approach which seeks to guide or direct activities or behaviours encouraging others towards shared goals and opportunities. This kind of leadership seeks to motivate parishioners to begin to think and behave in positive and constructive ways. Within modern Western nations, the marketplace of ideas and debate is an important forum for Catholics: If we do not compete with our ideas, energy and social programs, we risk invisibility to the wider population. Subsequently, there is no place in Catholic parishes for leadership that seeks to constrain or prohibit activities, goals or new opportunities. Particularly on dubious grounds such as "we have never done this before". The great challenge facing the Catholic Church is engagement with the wider world; we have the fullness of truth to offer. Christ himself dictates we do this. Leadership that constrains parish ideas and initiatives drives parishioners to think and behave in defensive ways.

Fundamentally, the role of a positive and forward looking leadership within a parish ensures a number of good relationship outcomes. There is a positive impact on parishioner energy and willingness to continue with tasks, others are empowered to give more of their time and ideas and parishioners feel that such leadership brings out their best.

No parish leadership can function without positive feedback. This impacts directly on the ability of parishioners to get along with others, to fight hard to remove obstacles and to continue to experiment with new ideas in the face of failure. There is no doubt that positive feedback creates an environment where a parish can increase communication, build affective teams and improve inter-personal relationships.

Unfortunately, some priests or "hands off" leadership groups do exactly the opposite. Parishes that exist within such an environment find reluctance in parishioners to participate and very low rates of effectiveness in the tasks that are undertaken. One of the strongest indicators of this negative environment for a parish is the lack of repair of sound systems, lighting, carpets and building facades. As in any home, mess, disorder and disrepair may be justified as "lovable" by people who have accepted this reality. The real truth is that you are driving away newcomers, who are unable to find things, but know clearly the message you are sending. Disorganisation and chaos will be read as laziness, sloppy intellectual life and a spiritual environment of near enough is good enough. Parishes that do not "claim" their personal space (their church) will not attract those looking for an energetic and vital future.

A key responsibility for any leadership team is the development, motivation and creation of new initiatives within the broad goals of the parish strategy. This means the formation of teams or units with oversight for particular roles or programs. The formation of effective teams is perhaps the most difficult of parish tasks, particularly if the priest or leadership team is unsure of their value. Overwhelmingly, teams only work productively when they are allowed to get on with their jobs. This does require maximising the autonomy of such groups. The role of the priest or larger leadership teams is not to task-manage goals or outcomes, but to strengthen communication and personal relationship, to help with problems and to maintain strong reporting channels. Any other approach, which results in maximising the control of these teams only results in an inhibited team which leads to low effectiveness and ultimate failure and long term disgruntled parishioners. The temptation to micro-manage parish teams almost always stems from the misunderstanding of priestly focus and wider leadership purposes. An individual priest or member of leadership team cannot undertake all roles within a parish structure. Indeed, this is the primary method of ensuring your parish does not grow. So what should be the priest's focus and the leadership team role?

Overwhelmingly, these key roles are related essentially to parish culture. Within many parishes almost no work or consideration is given to issues of culture, yet without a doubt, blockage, negativity, hostile individuals, or even an unbecoming atmosphere, stem from cultural issues. These will not be changed by a happy or jolly priest. They need serious consideration, discussion and action plans to change what is necessary. A sadder situation still is the high number of unsuccessful parishes where individual parishioners have no clue as to what the parish culture might be.

Parish culture is strongly related to past success or past failures. It is also generated by the attitudes of long serving parishioners and past clergy. In my experience parishes that have shown some ability to overcome past difficulties are often well placed to do so again. A story of resilience is your most vital asset. I visit a number of parishes that have rebuilt churches after fire; these parishes are currently the most successful in connecting to their local community and in sustaining and highlighting the unique aspects of their parish life. They are also the most successful at drawing new people into their Catholic life. Their culture has become one of "can do," no difficulty is too great, no individual is beyond help. These communities place the value of their culture above the changes of clergy or leadership teams and subsequently work from a motivation not driven by others. Whilst this is an ideal situation, developed from adversity, it is certainly possible for new clergy and leadership teams to develop this type of culture.

Primarily, this requires a constant message of overcoming obstacles. Even if a parish has no examples of such events, individuals do and personal stories and life experience can be used as strong motivators to form community. Every parish has a good number of individuals like this and it is important to highlight them – after all, they choose to attend your parish. Why? Because something of these characteristics can also be found in your collective life. It can be a significant bonding and growing experience for parish to hear these stories and importantly to identify with them.

I was fortunate to be a priest in two West London parishes, both of whom developed strong positive cultures from adversity. The first having been bombed in WWII had a particular mindset that the Luftwaffe couldn't finish us off, nothing can. This parish ran the largest children's and single parent support group in the region, all based on a culture that highlighted "if someone says we can't do something we will – after all the Luftwaffe couldn't defeat us!"

This is a wonderful culture as it stressed the ability of this parish to do and achieve any outcome it sets its mind to.

The second parish suffered a great deal of negative comment from other parishes, given its close proximity to a major prison in a rundown area of London. So whilst outsiders were negative about the region and its notorious prison, these factors were turned to positives by its people.

This parish developed a substantial prison visitation ministry and a viable ministry to wives and families of prisoners. This culture was founded strongly on "we are a parish that gets its hands dirty" and "no task is unachievable by us". The language, atmosphere and energy of the parish attracted large numbers of newcomers, all having bought into the "we are making a difference" culture of the parish.

This is a central role for both priest and leadership group: develop a positive "can do" culture, highlight and develop it and make sure it pervades all dimensions of parish life, from liturgy, youth groups, parish study groups and community programs.

The viability of your parish is directly related to the ability of clergy and leadership groups to attract and hold energetic people. Their skills and talent are of secondary importance. Strong and growing parishes have a "glue" that pervades the totality of their parish life, this begins with a "can do" culture, which attracts and stimulates energetic people and rests on a spirituality of serving "God calls us to make a difference to each other and our wider community". Naturally, all of this raises important questions for struggling parishes, if we are not doing this, what are we doing?"

IDENTIFY AND ENERGISE YOUR LEADERS: SYNOPSIS

- There is no such thing as a parish "gifted" with leadership. God provides but each parish must identify and nurture its people.
- Inspiring your parish comes first – leadership groups grow

from this.
- The first parish question must be "what do we want to achieve"? When that is decided leadership will follow.
- Parishes should not hand over responsibility for leadership to paid staff – they are add-on specialists, not core parish workers.
- Leadership roles should not be in the hands of only a few individuals – this leads to stagnation and lack of growth.
- Prescriptive leadership guides and directs parishioners towards shared goals, motivates and encourages people in constructive ways.
- Leadership that constrains or prohibits activities is destined to fail in the modern world of competitive ideas.
- Positive feedback impacts directly on the ability of parishioners to build affective teams and to improve interpersonal relationships within a parish.
- Poor parish leadership is first noticed in lack of repair to church buildings and general mess and disorder in parish undertakings.
- An important aspect of parish leadership is the formation of parish teams to initiate and manage projects – these should not be micro-managed by clergy or parish leaders.
- The key role of priests and parish leaders is the development of parish culture.
- Parishes with stories of overcoming difficulties and demonstrated resilience are more likely to have a positive and future driven culture.
- Parishes without positive "can do" stories can sometimes centre parish culture around inspiring individuals who attend their parish.
- The viability of a parish is directly related to the ability of clergy and leadership groups to attract and hold energetic people; this is unmistakably linked to the formation of positive parish culture.

15
EXCELLENCE RULES

New ventures start-up companies and improved technology often result in a surge of interest or sales for those individuals who have managed to establish a point of difference. If you are the only individual selling mangoes in an apple market you will certainly enjoy a period of unrivalled prosperity. However, this will not last. It will not be long before your point of difference will be copied, your model and philosophies adapted and you may well see new players on the block, who look like you, sound like you, are cheaper than you and ultimately take market share away from you. This is fundamentally what humans do: We copy. It is not linked to racial or national backgrounds, to male or female or any particular class or status. We learnt to walk and talk by copying, it is entirely natural behaviour and although we might not like it, good and original ideas will quickly be copied by others. This happens to churches as well and will impact on the way you conduct yourself, especially if you are seeking to grow your parish and enhance your contacts into the community. There will be church competitors in this space and some denominations or individual churches will certainly seek to resist your endeavours. Don't be naive about this, the world of ecumenism is as competitive as any other human activity, despite the fine words about co-operation, understanding and wishes of success. My strong advice is first get your own house in order, understand what your goals and objectives are and pursue them with determination. This does not mean cooperation with other churches is not possible, of course it is, and it can be done, but not from positions of weakness or with amateur misunderstanding or naivety.

The emergence of coffee shops in western society gives a useful example for modern churches, especially as we witness the emergence and strengthening of some denominations and the decay and death of others. On one level decay and death is related strongly to what you stand for: If you stop preaching the Gospel, forget to mention the centrality of Jesus and take up a myriad of social causes in its place, you have forgotten your core business and your reason for being – a sure recipe for disappointment, spiritual frustration and decline. There are large numbers of denominations, notably Anglicans, currently experiencing this ruin and decline.

Yet on the micro level of the individual church, decline may happen for other reasons as well. Take our coffee shop experience, you may have been the first and for a long time the only one in your retail area. Now you have been joined by several others. How do you maintain your vitality and loyalty of your customers when others may be cheaper, have faster service and a gimmicky presentation. Naturally, the first inclination is to tell your customers that you have better coffee, yours is superior in beans, in process and in flavour. Nevertheless, here you come up against an obvious problem. All your competitors will say the same thing and the standard coffee drinker for all their alleged sophistication usually can't tell the difference. When you are one of five or six and your product doesn't taste different to your competitors where do you go? The first and obvious mistake is to copy your competitors, search for your own gimmick and enter the world of novelty and passing "good ideas". Unfortunately, churches do versions of this as well.

So, what should your parishes do to maintain your integrity in who and what you are and concurrently to focus on growth.

Unquestionably, your primary focus must be based around excellence in all that you do. Excellence, integrity and honesty are the only things that can sustain the long-term commitment from parishioners that your parish requires for long-term growth.

Those charged with leadership of their parishes must understand the mutual obligation that is involved in such an arrangement. After all, it is disingenuous to complain of the disloyalty of parishioners, who may move to other parishes when your own offering is less than best or uneven.

These issues of excellence, integrity and honesty are at the heart of difficulties related to clergy sexual abuse. Parishes who have experienced this feel fundamentally stabbed in the heart, as abuse of this kind undermines the whole nature of the faith and raises the obvious question "If a parish can allow this to happen, how can anything they say be trusted"? These are life threatening issues that parishes must get right, yet it is not only clergy abuse which can challenge fundamental integrity. Issues to do with money, broken promises, dictatorial behaviour or lack of consultation on future plans can also elicit existential threats to parishes.

Many readers may be surprised to see a connection between excellence and integrity. This should not be the case. Excellence does not imply that you do everything well all the time, it equally implies that when you don't do things well, you admit these mistakes honestly and seek to change behaviour.

There are many parishes that are excellent, beautiful and inspiring in their liturgical practice, yet underneath people notice that something is missing. This is the honesty seen in openness, humility and acknowledgement that we can always do better. Excellence does not mean perfection, indeed perfectionism which may evolve into arrogance, heartlessness, or the inability to critique or laugh at yourself is another great enemy of Catholic mission. Excellence comes out of integrity. If parishioners can see that honesty and humility drive all that you do, they will quickly realise that your high standards are based on the right things.

Issues of excellence are easy to identify, yet somehow many parishioners still forget the regularity with which they occur. Excellence issues are at play in every point of contact you have with parishioners or the wider public. Have we all not ourselves been frustrated with staff from business or government services who are disrespectful or indifferent to our telephone calls and attempts to explain our difficulties. Have we not also considered moving companies or lodging complaints over the phone manner of some company representative? Yet, unbelievably, many parishes still imagine that not being responsive to phone calls or belittling people who wish their children baptised or seek to get married is somehow upholding standards? Is it excellence not to talk to newcomers as it must be someone else's job? Is it excellence when microphones, lights or TV screens don't work and elderly people can't hear your sermons? Is it excellence to produce news bulletins where nothing changes, apart from the Sunday readings for months on end. The way we conduct mass is important, it honours God correctly, but also honours those who have bothered, given up their time to come to be with your parish. Priests, commentators or readers who bumble through mass without care or preparation do significant damage to your parish reputation. I don't buy a car from a sloppy individual in a dirty showroom. Why should mass receive similar treatment unless I have no intention of really seeking to attract or encourage newcomers.

The follow-up of pastoral care is another important touch point of excellence and integrity. There is no excuse for slow or indifferent attention to those in need. Overwork is no excuse, absence on holidays is no excuse, and attending to other matters is no excuse. All these "excuses" may have contingency plans attached; yet you do fundamental damage to your parish and your own reputation when you cannot respond quickly to pastoral needs. The alternative is also the case, you win people over and they remember your efforts when you bother to give them the time of day, particularly in time of need.

In a parish world, cluttered with competitors, nobody expects your parish to be perfect, nevertheless, your parish should expect honesty and integrity that leads to your best efforts as often as possible.

EXCELLENCE RULES: SYNOPSIS

- Human beings copy each other regularly – if you do things well your parish will be copied – what will distinguish you then?
- Some parishioners will not have loyalty to you if they see the same thing offered closer to home.
- Successful parishes don't emphasise points of difference but excellence.
- Excellence is closely related to and driven by honesty and

integrity.
- Excellence is not perfection, but rather rests on humility and the importance of admitting and correcting mistakes and failures.
- Issues of excellence are in operation at every point of contact with both parishioners and the wider public.
- If you are sloppy or unprepared on the phone, at mass, or in care of your church, you do significant damage to your reputation.
- The quick follow-up of pastoral care requests from parishioners is a key indicator of your connection between honesty and excellence.

16

CHRISTIANS ARE DOERS WHO REVIEW THEIR RESULTS

The great problem that faces any organisation is moving from talk to action: Parishes are no different. In truth, the average parish is little more than a talk fest. More words, promises and good intentions are offered in the standard parish than perhaps any other human organisation. Both priests and people are guilty and the amount of verbal overkill in parish life is enough to deter anyone who really wants to make a difference. A central mark of a vibrant parish is that it is *filled with more doers than talkers*. "Go and make disciples of all nations" are the final words of the resurrected Jesus prior to his ascension. Unfortunately, he didn't stipulate on how this was to be done, but make no mistake, he firmly commanded that Christian culture and Christian life and mission are about "doing". If your parish does nothing, you do not deserve to be called followers of Christ. Whatever the excuses in priesthood or in parish life to do nothing is a scandal against the life and teachings of Jesus. *Christians are doers.*

In many parishes the operational culture is one of maintenance - we must maintain what we have, maintain our buildings, maintain our liturgical practices, maintain a priest in the presbytery. The attitude is almost always dressed up as a call to action: *It is not*. In fact, the destructive nature of such thinking can be seen in almost every parish that has been forced to partner, or share a priest with a nearby parish. Invariably the parish without the resident priest gets a subconscious message that "we are less important and we must hang on to what we have got". The great lack of faith here is to imagine that growth and revitalisation only happens to those who have a resident priest or to those who control the finances. New life comes from decisions to "do", it does not evolve from a decision to "hang-on".

The most important psychological undertaking of any parish talking about new growth is to resolve to be a parish of doers. It is important to recognise what this resolution will actually change. *Doing parishes commit themselves to measuring their goals and are not afraid to report regularly on their success or otherwise.*

This is a key way for a parish to maintain a doing focus, you must commit to measuring and reporting. It is impossible to activate drive, energy and a willingness to achieve, if you are afraid to report your outcomes. Yes, there is the possibility of failure, but this is not a central concern, the failure to begin or try is actually the surest path to death. Smart parishes don't mind failure because they recognise the series of benefits that have ensured from making a beginning. The new relationships formed, the sense of collegiality, the experience of working with Christ and the connections made into a local community. These are all growth outcomes despite the end result. No coach will bemoan the failure of a plan, as this can always be adapted, what is dispiriting is the failure to try.

What then do we need to measure?

1 **Trends in your area.** This includes changes in your locality. Are there new populations of people moving in or out? Are your partners contributing to their stated goals? Do you have a developing group of opponents? Are there possible new contacts to engage? Your parish environment constantly changes, only non-engaged parishes image that no changes occurs.

2 **Evaluation.** Are we doing what we said we would do? What is the ongoing feedback from participants, partners and leaders. Are we within stated time frames and budgets? Is the workload manageable or are there complaints of stress or unmet expectations.

3 **Performance of individuals, leaders and community partners.** Is everyone fully engaged – if not, what changes should be made? Are there changed circumstances in an individual's life or the life of your community partners? A significant measurement must always be around how the leadership group conducts

itself with the parishioners. Is there sufficient engagement? Are relationships friendly and respectful and most importantly are the parishioners using the leadership team as an effective forum for suggestions or constructive criticisms? The relationship between the leadership team and the wider parish must be under constant review and consideration as this group is the central avenue for gauging the health of any parish. One individual within a parish will not be able to understand the full range of issues, policies and possible solutions, this is a collective issue. A motivated and purposeful leadership group is essential to the organisation of a successful parish.

4 **Strengthening networks.** All parishes must have networks into the community. These relationships are your touch points beyond your parishioners. Some parishes imagine that these must always be liked minded groups who share your general values. Whilst this is important if you are planning to run programs together with such groups, it is also pertinent to remember that you are seeking to build trust. There may be some groups that don't like you, but could be relevant to your work and future goals. These relationships are built on calculated self-interest and emotional connections. Ensuring that your relationships with local community leaders are functioning and not allowed to decay after initial enthusiasm is vitally important to your long-term success in an area. It will constantly be the case that a number of individuals will be needed to nurture, grow and maintain these networks.

5 **Identify and diagnose problems.** All parishes are multi-faceted structures. This means that problems within a parish will always exist. Some issues will be caused by the decisions of your predecessors, or by those who have been alienated or sidelined in the past. Some individuals will not understand or agree with new ideas and goals that you set. In this sense leadership groups must be able to explore problems. Understand what you are facing and seek a consensus. Again, at every leadership meeting a review of problems, proposed solutions or ongoing hostilities must be considered. Strong leadership groups get on the same page quickly and recognise that agreed collective decisions are more likely to be seen as beneficial by parishioners. They de-

personalise anxiety or hostility to future paths. No leadership team should sacrifice one member as a scapegoat for decisions or problems. Diagnosing problems is an important aspect of successful leadership teams.

6 **Rates of participation.** Most parish programs will be designed to seek popular participation. We should normally be encouraging those who meet a certain criteria to participate as fully as often as possible. In one shocking example, I have seen a group of elderly female parishioners, who did not want a particular space used for youth group activities, attend that youth group. The desired sabotage occurred quickly with the loss of around 100 under 16 year olds being forced out of a parish space, ten years later this parish closed, as the behaviour of these post-70 year olds grew into local folklore.

Generally speaking, participation in your programs is a good indicator of agreement and success. Participation rates generally give programs a sense of legitimacy and should be reviewed by leadership teams from time to time. Those seeking to control outcomes with narrow parish visions and futures should be deterred by leadership groups from attending. It is hard to commence any new parish programs. Sabotage by those opposed must be dealt with swiftly.

7 **Giving.** A classic measure of success or failure in parish direction relates to giving. Parishioners will usually support financially those things they want to see happen within a parish: Indeed, they should be encouraged to do so, yet for such an outcome to evolve regular updates must be provided. These updates indicate your effectiveness, participation rates, improvements or changes and the atmosphere and joy in the group. If you are not prepared to provide such information then you can hardly expect ongoing financial support. Rightfully, parishioners vote with their pay packets – magically hoping financial support for your wonderful parish ideas will suddenly descend from heaven is wishful thinking. Reporting the truth, not spin, gives you a greater chance of long-term viability for your mission and vision.

8 **Lack of energy: Duration of Programs.** Almost always this is an area that is rarely monitored by parishes despite the fact

that all programs have a shelf life and many are go on too long. Leadership is exhausted, participants do so out of duty, costs are not always contained or some prestige may be attached to a founder or current advocate who finds it hard to let go. A good leadership group knows when to end something that has stopped working.

It is also the case that some programs can have a negative effect on the wider parish. It is not easy to consistently be responsible for changing, adapting and coming up with new ideas. Rapport and enthusiasm can be hard to maintain and lack of confidence or lack of energy can affect a group. Ending long term programs will sometimes cause hostility, as some individuals may have invested large amounts of their identity into such work. It is critical that those involved are firstly encouraged to contemplate, plan and to be energised over the next project, and then given rest. Ensuring your parish workers are not exhausted or crushed by constant programs gains significant respect for a leadership group. Firstly, a leadership team must value a contributor to parish life for who they are – not just for their skills. Naturally, if potential contributors to your programs feel valued, respected and cared for they will be more likely to take up future opportunities and have the energy to do them. Cessation or change to long-term programs must be a gentle process that focuses on the care of individuals concerned and should not be publically ended by implications of incompetence, financial irregularity or your lack of trust in the individuals involved. On occasions, these reasons may be at the forefront of the need to make changes, nevertheless, publically noting such causal factors makes it substantially harder to attract others to take their place. People generally do not wish to commit their time, energy or finances to things that have failed in the past through severe human error. The ability to end programs and care for those participating is an important sign of a healthy, well run parish. Priests or lay leaders who make announcements of things ending during Sunday notices without warning or preparation risk sending a strong message of their own incompetence.

9 **Conclusion.** Tracking, monitoring and constantly reviewing your

parish is notoriously difficult. Nevertheless, not to do so leads to the kinds of disasters that befalls many parishes. Community trust can be eroded, reputations trashed and exhausted parishioners move on or more likely just stop attending.

In the modern world, problems, blockages and overcommitted people are a fact of life. If you do not monitor your parish and its programs you risk having too many dimensions of chaos that guarantee healthy change cannot occur. There are significant numbers of parishes who have hit this wall and can do little beyond the basics.

In order to react effectively to change you must be able to pre-empt actions and gain the initiative – we must measure progress against our own plans and against best practice, in order to diagnose problems, draw affective conclusions and let others see the purpose and value of your actions.

Many parishes initiate programs with a great deal of energy, this is commendable, but only half a job. Interpreting and applying judgement, coupled with sound reasoning and respect are what ensures their acceptance and long-term future.

CHRISTIANS ARE DOERS WHO REVIEW THEIR RESULTS: SYNOPSIS

- New life in a parish comes from a decision to do, not to hang-on.
- Moving from talk to action is helped by a determination to review and analyse all that you do.
- Unsuccessful parishes don't review their work and consequently learn nothing.
- Successful parishes commit themselves to measuring their goals and are not afraid to report their successes and failures regularly.
- Drive and energy comes from review.
- What must you measure?
    (1) All changes in your area and community.
    (2) Are you doing what you said you would do.

(3) The performance of your leadership, a positive relationship to parishioners and a willingness to be a forum for suggestions or criticism is a key indicator of a successful parish.
(4) The strength of community networks.
(5) The ability to identify and diagnose problems.
(6) The rates of participation in your programs – those seeking to manipulate or sabotage programs must be challenged by parish leaders.
(7) The financial health of a parish is a strong indicator of general support. Reporting the truth, not spin, increases the long-term viability of your programs.
(8) Lack of energy and duration of programs. All programs and individuals involved should be monitored for exhaustion and de-motivation. This is an essential part of pastoral care towards parishioners. The ability to end dying programs without rancour is a key leadership skill.

- Proper review of your parish heads off future problems, maintains energised parishioners, increases respect and encourages parish longevity.

17
SETBACKS ARE NORMAL: BUILDING RESILIENCE

Possibly the most common experiences in parish life are of setbacks, disappointments and lack of progress. After all, Catholic parishes in the Western world, baptise and confirm thousands of people each year who are unable to sustain or develop their faith and stop attending. This should not be a surprise to us. Jesus predicted it, (Matthew 13.5) perhaps the more amazing phenomenon is that somehow most parishes imagine it shouldn't happen, consequently they don't prepare anyone, both within a parish and those recently joined that this is likely to be their experience.

Overwhelmingly, the number one comment of those who leave a parish is one of disappointment "somehow it didn't work for me", "perhaps Catholicism is not my thing", or "I just couldn't seem to connect or make sense of it". After the initial enthusiasm did we forget to tell newcomers about the twists and turns of faith life or even the large black holes that appear from time to time.

Parishes that do not prepare people for tough times as a normal experience actually have less chance of experiencing success, as it is only through struggle and understanding of failure that permanent success arrives. Unfortunately, many people leave the faith, the moment the first "mountaintop experience" declines and they have no ability to survive the "dry valley" below.

An attitude of resilience and persistence is an essential characteristic of any parish that expects to make a difference in peoples' lives and to project their life into the long-term future.

This resilience needs to be crystallised, talked about and displayed as a normal value that sits alongside the value of success in preparing for any endeavour. Concepts of struggle, setback, hard work and slow progress need to be incorporated into the journey.

Winston Churchill is rightly credited with the resilience and dogged never- surrender leadership, which enabled Britain to resist Hitler's Germany in World War II. What is often forgotten is that Churchill didn't magically arrive at this attitude on the day before a significant speech. The concept of never surrendering was already embedded in his personality and behaviour. "Success consists of going from failure to failure without loss of enthusiasm" and "continuous effort, not strength or intelligence is the key to unlocking our potential". Both of these quotes reveal a man who's general experience was one of incorporating setbacks, struggle and enthusiasm into an outlook of achieving success through hard work.

Modern parishes need exactly the same storehouse of resilience to meet the challenges being set forth in the modern world.

Intensity of purpose is absent in far too many parishes, people lose heart and go back to a minimalist offering. The irony of this is that paring down what you do to avoid failure, ensures that you have more. No effort is ever a failure; certainly many programs will fail to garner the support or participation you hoped for. Nevertheless, in working on your first project you will have mastered many of the techniques that can be used in your second attempt. The process of doing and mastering allows you to develop mental and physical structures that make putting new process and programs in place much easier. Setbacks generate a wealth of skills that can be used in the "next" venture. The most important phase in your parish vocabulary is "what next". Catholic understandings of God have never been based on a prayer life or a faith that is easy. God often appears to disappoint, sometimes to the point of causing non-belief, yet there is always a resurrection, (not always what we want) if we have eyes to see. Why would we imagine parish life is different. Death and Resurrection is God's central motif, our job is to prepare for it.

Many parishes will complain that diocesan officials or regional bishops are indifferent to their work, don't understand what they are trying to do and that this is the reason of slow progress or failure.

This is the basic excuse: we don't have the support or understanding of a higher authority, therefore we are unable to do what we really wish. This thought process is very damaging to achievement and to local success. Naturally diocesan authorities must be kept in the loop of your activities and progress, but why wouldn't you first imagine that your local initiative has something to offer the wider Church. Why is it not possible to imagine that your programs are cutting edge and that others would be inspired by your methodology and success? Subsidiarity is a fundamental Catholic political and social teaching, in its most basic formulation; it holds that social problems should be dealt with at the most immediate level consistent with a solution. This defines the role of central authority as supporting local initiatives and only performing those tasks which cannot be performed effectively at parish level. There is no excuse for blaming bishops or other diocesan staff for your inertia. Make your case and get on with it.

Apologies for inaction can take many forms; commonly many parishes will cite mitigating circumstances such as lack of resources or poor leadership for their lethargy. This is basic self-sabotage. All parishes have the necessary resources and people, provided you focus on self-reliance, start small, keep things sustainable and prioritise your effort.

Negative talk about your inability to do things will actually drive people further away. Often you will find financial backers and people willing to contribute their expertise only after you start. If you don't do anything how can any effective judgement on lack of resources actually be made. If you set your sights on what is achievable, the situation can still be transformed and developed into a great program. Trusting in Christ's resurrection is a good place to start.

Priests and leadership groups have a number of key tools to counter setbacks. Whatever else you do, you must keep the initiative. Failure, victimhood and mistakes are common human attributes, so common they are everywhere, in every life and in every parish or community. Yet they can plainly be managed, people do this every day, people overcome the most incredible setbacks, recovery from injury, or relationship breakdown, events in childhood, political betrayal, defeats in war - the list goes on and on. Controlling the initiative can be learnt, taught and implemented by people who at stages in their lives thought such changes were impossible, but they succeeded. The only non-acceptable position is to hand-over your initiative through hopeless and negative thinking. Twelve lost and hopeless disciples who encountered the resurrected Christ cannot be a bad model.

The recent history of the Catholic Church should teach another lesson. Cover-ups, denial and dishonest behaviour will absolutely lead to a worse outcome a few years down the track. Above all, such behaviour discredits Christ, Our Lady and all of your good people who sought to build something worthwhile in the name of your Church.

Admitting mistakes is essential to coping with setbacks and their aftermath. The hurt, pain and disappointment some individuals may feel at the collapse of a treasured programme, can be devastating. It is not reasonable to add to that pain. If you are not spiritually and morally prepared to admit mistakes and shoulder responsibility, don't start programs: you are only setting up your parish and community life for serious disappointment. Finally, it is important to remember that each parish program may have a new life and freedom in another form or under another group of leaders. Nothing is lost, provided your leadership team has the freedom to adjust its own thinking. Plasticity and rewiring are fundamental attributes of our human brain. Parish leadership groups must have the same attributes. You just need to give yourself time and the permission to think anew. Diversity of leadership, a willingness to "do" something, starting small and sheer bloody mindedness, are the ultimate controller of setbacks and developer of resilience.

SETBACKS ARE NORMAL – BUILDING RESILIENCE: SYNOPSIS

- Setbacks are a common human experience and pervade parish life.
- Parishes must prepare Catholics for "tough times" as a valid experience.
- Attitudes of resilience and persistence are essential for priests and parish leaders who expect to make a

difference.
- Setbacks and failures allow parishes to develop and master the physical and mental structures necessary for future success.
- Excuses are manifold, yet locals have control over their own destiny. Catholic subsidiarity emphasises the key role of local initiatives.
- Lack of resources or leadership are not valid mitigating circumstances. God provides what is necessary, each parish must highlight self-reliance. All sorts of individuals display resilience, your parish has these attributes as well.
- Admitting mistakes honestly and avoiding cover-ups is crucial for developing resilience – If you are not prepared to be trustworthy don't start parish programs.
- Individuals have brain plasticity and re-wiring capabilities. Parish leadership teams have the same attributes – Give yourself permission to think in new ways.

18

ONE SIZE DOESN'T FIT ALL: DIVERSITY THE BEGINNINGS OF GROWTH

Most parishes display a healthy schedule of mass or service times across Sundays and Saturday night vigils. The problem with this provision of worship opportunities is that they are nearly always the same. For parishioners only the timing has changed, the experience is groundhog day.

If you were to ask parishioners for honest feedback you might be surprised to hear that boredom and sameness are often highlighted as the greatest obstacles to regular attendance. This is usually packaged in an acceptable framework of lack of convenience, crowded activities with the children or difficulties in organising the family on Sundays, nevertheless justifiable reasons not to attend mass become stronger when mass formats, repetitive sermons and lifeless liturgy can be predicted.

No parish is exempt from this risk, yet many have given up on trying to vary their liturgy on even the most basic levels.

At the heart of this tedium is not the priests involved, the musical offering or the liturgical committee. It is a failure to understand the nature of mission. St Paul suggests Christians become all things to all people. He encouraged us to adapt, understand and fit in with all people, he did not mean offer the same thing to everyone. We have often forgotten this most basic missionary advice.

Children are different from teenagers, who are not the same as those in their 30's, families are different from those in their fifties, those in retirement are different again.

The aspirations, needs, hopes, values and finances of all these groups are radically different. That's why mature adults do not go to Justin Bieber concerts, or watch dramatic TV shows about the high school years. This is why under 20's are not drawn to Andre Rie'u concerts or spending their afternoon at high teas. At different times of our life, we are motivated by different desires and our tastes and interests change.

A parish community that is mono-cultural and only focused on one aspect of human life, by definition puts itself at risk of deterioration, being forced to merge with others and ultimately closure. This is not hard to see in action. If your services are predominantly attended by over 60's, you have a problem. If somehow you do not consider this a problem and imagine all will be well, then I would draw your attention to the Anglican Church in Australia, or the Episcopalians in America as dying churches who are unable to adapt. Without diversity you will weaken and perish and you deserve to do so as you have failed to act on your call of mission, "Go and make disciples of all nations, baptising them in the name of the Father, the son and the Holy Spirit (John 20).

Parishes that continue to take a generalist approach and do not have specialist avenues, catering for a wider variety of parishioners, risk stagnation through boredom.

I am not suggesting the re-invention of the rock mass from the 1970's, but I am advocating a subtle adaptation of mass frameworks to include and attract more children, families and under 25's. These two groups are notoriously difficult to attract and hold, and it will be necessary to undertake a great deal of pre-planning, thinking of different individuals in leadership (readers, commentators etc) and of gaining a commitment from families to support these new ventures. Those parishes connected to Catholic schools may even consider moving mass venues into the environment which is safer and more familiar to your newcomers: the school itself. I have seen mass congregations grow within a school that is only 200 metres from the church. You may ask, why would you bother, but this reluctance of parishes to adapt does not consider the issues of culture, familiar surroundings and ownership. I would rather have 200 children coming to mass in my school hall, when none of them will attend the church only 200 metres away. This is certainly only a preliminary step and much teaching should go on in relation to the beauty of full community mass. Nevertheless, let's get the first step happening before lamenting that children, families or young people won't attend our services.

The first stage of planning for parish growth is to recognise that one size doesn't fit all. Leadership teams then need to think about what types of mass they may want to offer and where. All parishes must resist an indolent attitude which suggests everyone must come to you. Where else within your parish boundaries can mass be held that will bring local people along with your goals for growth? Getting out of your church building, even into the open air for special occasions, signals the possibility of attitude change and a fresh approach. There will always be lots of objections and reasons not to do this, which brings me to a second key point in growing parishes. You need a single, repeatable and recognisable narrative so that your parishioners can understand why you are changing and what you hope to achieve. This narrative may be something like, "our parish is going into its community" or "we are a parish of our community". These are the narratives you promote when making change. There is no point in making an imposed change, without explanation, in the hope that parishioners will understand your reasoning: they won't. Firstly, and most importantly, you need an agreed narrative that most parishioners have understood, if not agreed with, then you make change under this "umbrella", but never without a narrative!

It is also important that a parish narrative has a timeframe. Parishioners must see that you are energetic and prepared to "move" on your goals. To talk about trendy narratives, without action, only weakens the possibility of the idea actually working. In the same way, you must be prepared to say this is our "narrative" for two years and at the end of this we will review, modify, abandon or enhance the activity promoted under its umbrella.

Another prime aspect of parish growth is building local talent. Many parishes lament the alleged lack of local talent and skills in parishioners or their friends. Let's be clear, no parish has all that it needs sitting in pews waiting to be enthused by a priest or leadership team. Before you can build anything, you must have an outcome or program in mind. Once this is established it is possible to search for the capabilities, support and equipment you need from within your parishioners. Parishes that claim they lack talent or support are almost always asking little from their people in the first place. Developing a program, asking for support and searching for missing talents, also "hardwires" your parishioners that this is something you will be asking again in the future. It conditions your parish environment, to see themselves as employing their skills, adding value to their faith, but mostly importantly it builds the base of talent and skills you need for continued future growth.

There can be a tendency in some parishes to see parish life and work as a form of social work. This is not the prime task of your parish: worship, faith formation prayer, teaching and learning to love each other are our primary Catholic responsibilities. Nevertheless, a parish that does nothing within its community, fails to respond to needs or only seeks to serve itself is at risk of corroding the very faith it purports to support. Our Catholic life together is formed and actioned by service to others, "whatever you do to the least of my brothers you do to me" (Matthew 25,31-46). Therefore, there must be in each parish a dimension of community service. Without this dimension we are also failing to live our faith to the full, as Christ commands.

It is disconcerting to witness the large numbers of parishes who have largely lost this dimension of their faith. Naturally, there may be many good reasons for this. There is certainly a tendency in Western society to transfer accountability for programs and social works to super-agencies who provide such services on a large scale. Yet, it is my strong belief that parishes which allow themselves to become "funding avenues" for these mega agencies are inadvertently contributing to their own demise.

Another motto important for the local parish is "your growth equals your connection to your community: no connection means no growth". Unfortunately, there are too many parishes who register growth and mission in terms of collecting new parishioners from nearby parishes. This is not growth, it is theft! Growth and mission have a primary purpose of making new Christians and engaging those historically unconnected to you in the life of your parish.

Successful parishes measure that against the impact and connectedness they have with their local communities, once this is effectively established it may be the case that mass attendance and parish growth also occur, but first make the connections in honesty and trust.

In the first instance, you should consider searching for community projects that are not duplicated by others. Avoiding turf wars with others is important, but more powerfully you begin the process of establishing your own identity around the programs you run. It is vitally important that you become known in your region for your work in particular areas. New parish people must be able to clearly identify you with that work, only then can you talk about influential community engagement. Identifying, planning and operating in your own niche market is a seminal way of entering into community social work.

Diversity is also strengthened by having the humility to admit you do not have all the resources or leadership you need to run a program. Therefore, be prepared to engage outside experts for help. Such individuals potentially bring a new set of eyes to your programs and raise possibilities you may not have considered. This process also telegraphs to both the wider community and your parishioners that you are serious about making a real difference and maintaining viability over the long period. Parishes that start new ventures, without community trust, often fold quickly, but unfortunately pass on the message to the community that the Church is a bunch of amateurs, without knowledge or foresight. Don't be afraid to find advisors, use them and encourage them to further promote your work amongst their contacts.

Finally, it is of paramount importance to trust the leadership group you have established to both run the programs and make the community contacts. This kind of person to person contact is often heartfelt and insightful and can be beneficial for your parish. Community connections don't need to know the priest or your leadership team, just allow these contact relationships to naturally occur. Friendships are born from this, more programs will be likely to occur and parish growth will happen by osmosis.

ONE SIZE DOESN'T FIT ALL: DIVERSITY THE BEGINNING OF GROWTH: SYNOPSIS

- Many parish activities are mono-cultured and create boredom.
- Parishioners cite boredom as an obstacle to regular mass attendance.
- Individuals in their 20's, 40's and 60's and above are radically different from each other and need parish mass and events that suit their tastes – one size does not fit all.
- Parishes that offer a generalist approach and do not have specialist avenues risk stagnation and no growth.
- Parishes must at least consider different programs and masses, for children, families and under 25 year olds.
- Parishes must have a single narrative under which "ownership" of new programs, events and changes can occur. Imposed change doesn't work and leads to resistance.
- Parish narratives must have a concluding timeframe to encourage "moving - on goals" and to allow for a period of review, modification, abandonment or enhanced activity.
- Alleged lack of talent is not an excuse for inaction – most parish leadership has never established workable programs on which to ask for parishioners support.
- Developing programs "hardwires" parishioners to expect to be asked to help and use their skills in parish settings. This "program environment" builds your base of parishioner skills for future use and growth.
- There must be a balance between worship, prayer and social programs in each parish. Overbalancing towards any one area risks self-serving indulgence and lack of growth.
- Parishes that have stopped community service risk disconnection with that community.
- Parishes that only "fund" large social work agencies inadvertently bring about their own demise. Your growth equals your connections to your community. No

connections mean no growth.
- Parishes beginning community projects should seek "niche" opportunities, to allow your parish to become known and associated with this work.
- Non parish community members must be able to identify your parish with your specific programs – only when this happens can parishes claim influential community engagement.
- Diversity is strengthened by parishes having the humility to engage outside help.
- Outside "expertise" increases community confidence that parishes know what they are doing.
- Parishes must be prepared to encourage new one-on-one relationships between parishioners and community helpers.
- Parishes that trust their leaders of community programs, will increase community friendship, collaboration, future programs and parish growth by osmosis.

19
THE GLOBAL PARISH

To envision the future of any parish or diocese is fraught with hazard and risk. Nevertheless it is possible to make general projections based on current directions and trends. Our modern world already experiences rapid change and a significant history of disruptive technologies, political upheaval and the habitual occurrence of phenomena which were once thought to be impossible. Which one of us could ever have predicted the internet, the fall of communism or the September 2001 attacks in New York.

Concurrent with its divine mission and purpose, the Church is also a social organisation. Whilst the intricacies of parish life in the future are unknowable, the framework in which future parishes will evolve can be seen in conditions that currently exist.

The modern world seems to be driven by four key phenomena which must be considered by the contemporary parish as it seeks to study its place in the World.

There is no doubt that population growth, increased urbanisation, littoralization and increasing connectedness are trends that are expanding at an intense rate. Population growth and urbanisation are intimately related - not only is the world population expected to grow from today's 7 billion to around 9 billion in 2050, but almost all of this new growth will reside in cities.

In 1800 only 3% of humanity lived in cities with over one million people, by the year 2000 47% of global population was urbanised and by 2050 approximately 75% of the world's population will live in cities.

This unparalleled urban expansion is occurring overwhelmingly in poorer parts of the world, in Asia, Latin America and Africa. Already in these locations infrastructure is under severe strain often resulting in collapse and crisis in hospitals, schools, food and water supplies and lack of governance in large urban regions. The addition of gang related crime, extortion and terrorist activities have increased the menace to public safety and national security.

Alongside, this dramatic increase in urbanisation is another widespread circumstance, which finds this concentration of new cities predominantly located in coastal areas (littoralization). Already in 2012 85% of the earth's population lived within 100 kilometres from the sea and 78% of large cities are on the coast.

The rapid growth in population and urbanisation will also continue to act on the structural integrity of parishes for many decades to come. Many parishes will continue to grow numerically and those located on outer spheres of larger cities will be required to increase the geographical dimensions of their parish boundaries. Increasingly, this will see considerable numbers of non-Christians, both of other faiths and those secularised, living close to parish churches. The days of displaying mass times on notice boards and expecting significant attendance figures will continue to lessen. Of primary importance will be local mission activities, specifically designed for the people of your district, appealing across age groups and social difference and all focusing on the local parish environment. Mission will become the imperative of the future parish, given the large numbers within parish boundaries, the higher percentage of non-Christians and the likely erosion of social and community adherence. The future of Christianity is likely to see a withdrawal from centralisation and a return to the distinctiveness and importance of the local parish.

Pastoral initiatives at a local level will also need to be radically enhanced. As greater numbers of individuals and families are experiencing, loneliness, breakdown, mental illness, suicide and significant long-term disruptions in employment. Friendship groups and relationships will see greater opportunities for parish communities to provide such services. Yet, most significantly, the need for community, care and a sense of belonging will also intensify as governmental services are stretched beyond their coping capacities. The local parish, which forms home groups, pastoral care groups and can provide a sense of Catholic identity, will, in my view, become the primary community in urban conclaves of the future. The parish community of 2016 must have a vision of itself which is able to adapt and strengthen their own local initiatives with a view to the role of the parish in 2066.

Since the 1990's another phenomenon has rapidly developed, and conjoined to the proliferation and intensity of urban populations. This is the increasing importance to connectedness through networks, notably those of the internet, satellite TV and mobile phones which are both inexpensive and of high quality.

The desire for connectedness appears to live at the heart of human nature. Humanity is designed for community which increases health, happiness, sense of well-being along with providing greater opportunities for socialisation, work, friendships, relationships and family development. The movement of large populations from rural areas to urban fringes has been largely driven by this desire for greater access to global and local systems of exchange.

The Catholic parish system has been slow to understand and capitalise on the huge advantages that can come from such connectedness. Another obvious example rests within the migrant communities that now reside within many western parishes. These country to country connections are usually very weak because there has not been an "intentionality" to establish, develop and enhance them, yet such opportunities are virtually unlimited.

If we accept the notion that the development of leadership teams and enhancing ways of connecting for your community is essential to the future of your parish community, then why would you continue to be limited to what's available within your local region?

Could a parish not consider exchanging or engaging an overseas parish with the intention of establishing the formation of such a team. The idea of importing a short-stay mission team to help your parish unpack and begin to apply missionary endeavours on a local basis is not impractical, if such activity is prioritised. This possibility exists on a number of levels, perhaps internationally and interstate, but certainly within provinces and other parts of your own city.

Many parishes experience difficulties with acquiring and sustaining the skills necessary for mission and ministry. Corporate organisations consider the need for change, renewal and new ideas to be a priority when lack of growth and decline become normality. The Catholic Church with its global and intra-national networks is in an excellent position to consider such options.

Catholic parishes in non-Christian countries could certainly consider parish to parish mission activities as an excellent method of boosting awareness and interest amongst uncommitted locals. At the parishioner to parishioner level, opportunities for exchange teaching, the sharing of ideas and energy are unlimited. The commercial Airbnb company offering short-term living quarters, breakfast and networking opportunities for those unable to book a hotel is certainly possible of duplication on a Catholic parish exchange model.

It is also conceivable that youth exchanges, offering young Catholics (particularly those in circumstance where Catholic communities may be undersized) opportunities to temporarily join thriving communities, providing insight and encouragement that can be applied in the home community.

Critical significance should be given to exchanges on a parishioner level that offer a host parish opportunities to benefit from the teaching skills, or program knowledge of skilled parishioners with an aim to local duplication and implementation. Parishes that are determined to establish youth groups or young families support structures, but lack the knowledge and expertise, can benefit considerably from the presence of skilled and motivated lay people with understanding of successful program implementation. There is no reason why a parish or diocese should feel unable to provide such leadership skill expertise in the current global age. Models that encourage sister to sister parish exchanges, adopt parish models, or school to school and youth hosting are all ideas that have worked in other cultural and commercial areas. The considerable advantage for Catholic parishes is the noticeable opportunity for parishes to benefit on a corporate level, not just for the individuals concerned. In a global age, where mission has become both more important and has a renewed focus on local initiative, these inter-parish support and teaching networks cannot be ignored.

A common issue concerning many nations in the modern era is unemployment, notably youth unemployment. Issues of job creation, training and providing young Catholics with a future is at the heart of the Catholic message. If we are unable to provide young people with secure lifelong employment, then we should not be surprised to find that the "Catholic goods" of marriage, family, buying a house, educating your children and sustaining parish culture and identity are harder for modern young people to sustain. The Catholic life, initiative, spirit and enthusiasm are premised on the necessity of secure employment. Catholics must be at the forefront of securing our young people with futures invested in vital employment.

The possibilities of parish engagement with young people in the provision of employment are endless. Most parishes have substantial short-term work opportunities in and around their church plant. Additionally, many parishes have an abundance of retired and skilled parishioners who are looking for ongoing ways to give back to their community and local parish. Why not consider a parish program operated under parishioner guidance, in providing entry level skills, encouragement and a connection to the local Catholic parish community. These programs could be operated by locals, yet parishes without such skills may consider engaging small groups from another parish. The enthusiasm, sense of pride and mission opportunities may well be decisive for a local parish, particularly ones that are burdened with negativity and a sense of decline.

The parish of the future has immense opportunities for mission and engagement, particularly in a world of increasing population and urbanisation. In a world with less ability to provide social services to all its citizens, parishes must consider their future mission and growth not only in terms of spiritual practice, but also in the vital stepping stones of providing community, education, employment, youth activities, counselling, aged support and a whole new range of community engagement. We neglect this at severe risk to our mission and future. The teaching of Jesus that Catholicism will be known by its fruits will never have more importance than in forthcoming years.

THE GLOBAL PARISH: SYNOPSIS

- The future parish will be strongly influenced by four key drivers - increased population, urbanisation, littoralization and greater connectedness.
- Rapid future population growth and urbanisation will force parishes to change current models of operation.
- Local missions and social support will require a stronger parish focus, given greater diversity of urban population, an increase in non-Christians and higher youth unemployment.
- Mission activity must have a specific local content and culture: centralisation will decrease and local distinctiveness increase.
- Connectedness must be "intentionally" embraced by a parish.
- The Catholic parish has been slow to take advantage of urban connectedness. The connections between Catholic migrant communities could be used to establish short-term mission teams, clergy exchange, youth exchanges and the acquisition of skills in youth and family work from short-term visits of parishioners with particular expertise.
- Youth unemployment is a global difficulty which needs cooperation between Catholics and the local parish levels.
- Immense opportunities for future growth and mission are available to Catholic parishes prepared to re-orientate their focus to embrace community engagement and support.

20

WORK, FAMILY AND CATHOLICISM
WHAT REALLY DRIVES YOUR PARISH

Catholicism has always highlighted the centrality of work and family as two key planks on which much of the faith depends. Unfortunately in recent years the prominence previously given to the importance of finding a job and maintaining steady work has decreased substantially in Catholic sentiment. Whilst the significance of the family has been maintained as a primary Catholic standpoint, how these two convictions can be promoted, sustained and developed in the parish environment is usually given little or no promotion.

Any parish wishing to re-energise its connections to the wider community and its own lethargic or lapsed base needs to consider how it might promote work and family initiatives to the forefront of its mission and wider public persona.

The case for work should be an easy one to construct. However, this is not always the case as we have largely forgotten the importance of work on all of the Catholic "goods" in faith and society. If I am unable to gain employment, how can I reasonably expect to form a serious relationship or enter into marriage? The sacrament of marriage in the modern world is premised on a reasonable measure of consistent wealth and prosperity. Without employment how can a young couple seriously consider such lifelong commitment? Additionally, without employment, my chances of purchasing my own home remain illusory. The purchase of a home is still the bedrock of wealth for most Western couples.

Lacking the financial strength to marry or build a home must ensure that the birth of children, their schooling and their security in a stable family environment is radically diminished. Statistical support from Western societies bears this out. When youth unemployment is high, marriage and the birth of children is delayed or abandoned, opportunities for Catholic schooling and teaching are harder and the desire of Catholic parents to attend mass and include themselves and their children in the life of a parish becomes more complex and exacting.

There is now a tendency for Catholics to rely on bishops or diocesan officers to make significant public statements surrounding these issues. However, many media outlets and the wider community have stopped listening to top down pronouncements. Now is the time for local initiatives to be driving a revival of the importance of work and family for the local community and most importantly for the health of the local parish.

It is my strong contention that each local parish should be engaged in the creation of employment in the local area, especially for young people. This is an objective that offers a reasonable prospect of success. Local projects do not need to be grandiose or of unending duration, but they do need to engage your parish in some coal-face activity with individuals who actually live in your region. What is to stop most parishes offering maintenance jobs to encourage younger people to undertake their first job. What is to stop a parish investing in the improvement of its own hall or church building, painting, cleaning, gardening, minor building, concrete laying etc. These are all jobs every parish needs to be engaged with. Why not try to create a system where such jobs may be overseen by skilled parishioners and at the same time offer young unemployed their first step in the job market. The encouragement experienced by individual participants is a powerful motivator in overcoming difficulties and becoming resilient and worthwhile contributors to society. The connections gained by the parish also offers parishioners the possibility of knowing young locals and encouraging them to connect to the parish over a longer period. These programs are self-fulfilling if you make connections and do something for others more connections and benefits will flow to your parish as well.

Mary Eberstadt, in her book *How the West really lost God* offers some important challenges to current thinking regarding secularisation and the reasons the Catholic faith seems to be struggling to engage with its own communities.

Eberstadt dismantles conventional explorations for the decline of churchgoing, especially those implying that people in becoming more educated and prosperous became more sceptical of Church teachings. The argument that wealthy and smart people have less use for Catholicism is deeply flawed and not supported by facts. After all, if this was correct we would naturally expect poorer and less educated people to be more religious. The statistics suggest the opposite, Catholicism is overwhelmingly a middle class phenomenon, with additional strong clusters of adherence amongst upper class. A church that is for "the poor" may sound principled, the reality is that adherence to Catholicism is no longer working-class or uneducated in nature.

In a similar manner, devotion to Catholicism has been described by modern atheists, Richard Dawkins and Christopher Hitchens as signifying an imagined consolation on the part of Catholics. This is a reworking of the old anti-Catholic ideas of Catholicism as a soothing delusion in the face of mortality, suffering, deprivation and unpredictability of life. Naturally, as any Catholic can attest, the costs and demands of the faith can be difficult, not only the disruption to life by the demands of observance, but also the distinct possibility in many countries of persecution, restraint of education and employment and even individual or communal martyrdom. The current severe persecution of Christian communities in Islamic societies gives further lie to the soothing nature of Catholicism.

Finally, Eberstadt notes another common explanation for the decline of commitment to Western Catholicism. This theory points to the disruption of two World Wars fought on European soil in the twentieth century as eroding belief in the nature of God as "good and loving". Certainly the destruction of World Wars I and II would seem to highlight the darkness of the human heart. Nevertheless, this theory does not account for the substantial secularisation occurring prior to the European wars. The considerable problem for this theory is its statistical bankruptcy, particularly after World War II which witnessed a substantial surge in mass attendance, particularly in the years 1945-1958. The catastrophe of wars seems to call forth greater faith not less.

Eberstadt proffers another solution to the deterioration that has occurred in Catholic parishes at the onset of the 1960's. This interpretation goes to the heart of Catholic teaching and practice. Eberstadt notes that "vibrant families and vibrant faith" go hand in hand. The fortunes of Catholicism are closely related to the fortunes of the intact, married family. The statistical evidence strongly indicates that unmarried people without children are less likely to attend mass than married people, or married people with children.

It appears that the Church is strongly attractive to married people for a number of reasons. In the first instance they are certainly likely to find other couples, similarly engaged in the ups and downs of family life, nevertheless on a deeper level it appears other factors are strongly in play. Firstly, children drive parents to church in the sense of encouraging them to transmit moral and religious precepts and secondly, men are more likely to remain within Catholicism with the advent of children and family life.

This significant link between maintaining and developing the faith and family life cannot be downplayed or ignored by parishes. This is particularly of note for children and men, two groups in the recent decade which have begun to show signs of fluctuation and wavering.

It will also have been noted in many Western parishes that teenagers and individuals in the early twenties are also notably absent from mass. Statistically this is also related strongly to family life, as most evidence suggests that young people still living at home are less likely to stop attending mass. The experience of living in a family seems to make people more receptive to mass attendance and maintaining their faith into adulthood.

If we accept the premise, that the family is a principle driver of the faith, indeed that Catholicism is vitally dependent on strong married families, then we must in the local parish do as much as we can to make our masses, our groups and our offering as attractive to the family as possible. This must mean the consideration of specific masses designed for local families. The argument that the modern family has many other commitments from school, sports and activities cannot be allowed to take hold as a parish mantra. Statistically, the family is the key and most important driver in the future viability of your parish - to cede this position to a sporting club or a hobby will place a life threatening knife to the throat of your parish.

The centrality of the family to Catholic life is further underlined when the fertility rates of Western society are considered. These have been dropping in Europe since the late 1700's with the additional new phenomenon of around 1/3 of European adults aged 20-34 years living together without contracting a marriage. It is now possible to note a quadrangular connection that impacts on Catholicism. As fertility rates in the West decline, cohabitation increases, marriage declines and attachment to Catholicism weakens.

This phenomenon commenced firstly in the historically Catholic nation of France, but can be witnessed clearly in the recent challenges to Catholicism in Ireland where the decline in mass attendance is the steepest in Europe from 91% in 1973 to 18% in 2011. This dramatic decline in Ireland did not transpire in a vacuum, but was prefigured by an equally steep decline in the family.

Underlying this sharp family decline, expressed in an increasing unwillingness to enter into marriage and commit to having children is the development of the contraceptive pill. This advance in contraceptive technology and its accompanying sexual revolution has seen the weakening of family bonds for both men and women, but especially for men where marriage was no longer linked to sex, increasing a loss of interest in marriage and a devaluing of Catholic teaching on family and moral matters.

The response of many non-Catholic denominations to these new family attitudes was to construct a Christianity with allegedly a "more understanding and inclusive morality." The acceptance of divorce and contraception, the embrace of cohabitation in place of marriage and the recent acceptance of homosexuality have all driven substantial doctrinal changes in these churches, not previously permissible in Christianity's, two thousand year history.

In retrospect, these adaptations have been self-destructive. Within all protestant denominations, attendance numbers are down, finances are collapsing, the young have left and families are no longer found in these congregations. Undoubtedly, relaxing traditional teachings has hastened the decline of those denominations that made such change.

Whilst the Catholic response to these family challenges has not been one of compromise, we must nevertheless recognise that the health of the Western family is not in good shape. Fewer people are having children and those that do are experiencing greater difficulty in maintaining intact two parent families for children to grow up in. Institutional substitutes for the family from baby day care to nursing homes are in usage in greater numbers than at any stage of Western history. The advocates for alternative family arrangements are stronger and more hostile to the Catholic view of family than ever before and the substantial numbers of broken homes pose a new difficulty in mission and evangelism to people who may be hostile in receptivity to Catholic teaching.

Nevertheless, there are tremendous opportunities for Catholic parishes, strengthened by the Holy Spirit to engage with broken families, single parents, fatherless and lonely children. The state has proven unable to undertake such work effectively and is rapidly withdrawing economic support from many of these families. This process will only increase in future years and present the Catholic Church with opportunities to engage, restore and heal such families in ways that go beyond a fortnightly payment. The essential nature of the Catholic parish is one of mercy and nurture, the possibilities for programs that support single parents are endless. Practical help in washing, child minding, financial advice and emotional support are now things that parishes must consider. Engagement with our communities must be practical and local. Each parish has hundreds of individuals who could benefit from such programs. In a similar way, the absence of fathers has opened a huge gateway for local parishes. The need for substitute fathers and grandfathers, taking an interest in local young boys without role models is enormous.

The Catholic Church has historically been known for its fierce defence of underprivileged or socially excluded Catholics, particularly in regions where Catholics have not formed a majority. Now is the time for us to re-direct our endeavours wholeheartedly to the needs of families, single mothers or fathers and children who need support. Our mission and caring responsibilities have not changed, we just need to think anew.

WORK, FAMILY AND CATHOLICISM
WHAT REALLY DRIVES YOUR PARISH: SYNOPSIS

- Work and family are two key planks central to catholic life and practice.
- Finding and maintaining work is the basis for marriage, family, children, Catholic schools and mass attendance.
- Pronouncements from Catholic bishops or officials have become irrelevant in modern media – local parish work initiatives must drive Catholic renewal.
- Local parishes have substantial opportunity to offer small scale work to local young people.
- Catholic decline is not the result of "traditional" secular arguments against religious belief, such as wars, affluence, or improved education.
- Catholic deterioration mirrors the decline of the family. Catholic health is closely related to the maintaining of intact married families.
- The formation of families appears to increase mass attendance in greater numbers than for single people or defacto couples. A strong indicator for family mass attendance appears to be a desire to transmit moral and religious precepts.
- Men are more likely to maintain faith practice when part of an intact family with children.
- Catholic parishes must be attractive to families and children for their survival.

- Parishes must not cede their family connection to sporting clubs or family hobbies.
- Western fertility rates are in decline, cohabitation is rising, marriage is being contracted later in life.- All these factors weaken Catholicism.
- Contraceptive technology has weakened men's commitment to marriage. If sex is more available outside marriage, men's interest in marriage is devalued along with Catholic teaching on family and morality.
- Christians denominations which have "adapted" to these circumstances have declined quickly: removing moral standpoints is self-destructive.
- Catholics have maintained family attendance in a broad sense, but must acknowledge the crisis facing the family is severe. Catholic families have also suffered significant stress and turmoil.
- Western Government are unable to financially support large numbers of broken families and are withdrawing benefits and support services.
- The Catholic Church has significant opportunities to provide practical programs supporting single parents and fatherless children in particular.
- The Church will need a willingness to engage in different ways with local families to support and strengthen existing families and to nurture those suffering divorce, separation or absent fathers. A willingness to move beyond "comfort zones" will be necessary.

About the Author

Fr James Grant MAICD BA BTh GDip IS GDip Comp ST
GDip Trauma Counselling

Born in Adelaide, and schooled in Essendon, Victoria. Fr James joined the Commonwealth Police in 1977 with an initial posting in Canberra. He has qualified as a martial arts instructor in Brazilian Jiu Jitsu, scuba diving and played first grade cricket for Northcote.

Fr James undertook theological studies at Melbourne University, graduating in 1984. Appointed to the UK as an associate priest, He became one of London's first white vicars to minister to the expanding West Indian community Fr James initiated his first interfaith gatherings in west London following the Brixton riots, after which he was appointed on short term placement to Berlin (west Germany) in 1988 and Budapest in 1989.

Fr James returned to Australia in 1989 where he was Senior Chaplain at Geelong Grammar School for seven years, followed by two years at St Michael's grammar and six years at The Peninsula School. He was noted for his pastoral care with a focus on martial arts, football and cricket as methods for building confidence in students.

In 2004 he was appointed a parish priest at St Stephens Richmond , then in 2005 Melbourne's first team vicar for the new parish of Jika Jika in Melbourne's north with responsibility for a large Sudanese refugee community. As Parish priest for the Preston area, he was a strong advocate for the Nuba people, of Sudan, who are experiencing genocide. He has built two schools in Northern India.

Fr James founded Chaplains Without Borders in 2004 to initiate new ventures into corporate and community organisations, and CWB grew to be Australia's largest chaplaincy service within 2 years. He went on to be appointed as the world's first chaplain to the casino industry in 2006 (Crown Enterprises Australia) a position he still retains.

As a leading traditionalist within the Australian church, Fr James supported the development to the Anglican Ordinariate in Australia and served on the national committee as secretary 2010-2011. Fr James was received into the Catholic Church and ordained as a Catholic Priest in September 2012 as a foundational priest for the Australian Ordinariate. In 2012 he was appointed National director for Ordinariate schools and to the Ordinariate governing council.

Fr James has continued to develop missions including Catholics in Business 2012 and Catholics in Mission and renewal in 2013. His CYA (Catholic Youth Academy) youth program works through Crown casino to develop confidence in de-motivated young Australians and find work placements within Crown. In 2013 he co-established the Renewal Centre.

He is the first Chaplain appointed to an A league soccer club in Australia at the largest Australian club, Melbourne Victory. He is involved with 9MM pistol competition and is completing PPL training for Helicopters

In 2015 Fr James established the Father James Grant foundation, implementing programs for de-motivated young Australians and the resurgence group a team designed to help parishes re-energize their community life.

www.chaplainswithoutborders.org
www.catholicsinbusiness.org
www.thefatherjamesgrantfoundation.org
www.theresurgence.org

www.ingramcontent.com/pod-product-compliance
Lightning Source LLC
Chambersburg PA
CBHW030141170426
43199CB00008B/160